GCSE Media Studies Revision Guide

An In-depth Explanation of All Media Studies Terminology

For All Examination Boards

Copyright©Z.Logan2023

Contents

GCSE Media Studies Examination

Terminology

TV

Advertising and Marketing

Magazines

Online and Social Media (podcasts)

Film

Music and Video

Radio

Newspapers

GCSE Media Studies Examination:

For specific Exam Board Specifications please visit your individual school's examination board.

This book deals with over-arching themes of the GCSE Media Studies with specific focus on terminology, content and important details you should know.

It can however, be used for all examination boards to prepare for all GCSE Media Studies Assessments.

At the back of this book are a number of sample similar GCSE Media Studies Examination questions created that can serve to point you in the direction of where you may be weak in your studies and where you need to study more.

Wish you all the best in your Studies.

Good Luck!

Media Studies is at GCSE Level

Media Studies at GCSE level is an academic subject that focuses on the critical analysis and production of media content. It typically covers topics such as advertising, film, television, news, and digital media, and explores how these forms of media are created, distributed, and consumed.

Students learn how to analyze and deconstruct media messages, as well as develop skills in media production, such as filming and editing. The subject also covers key concepts and theories related to media; such as representation, audience, and genre, and encourages students to think critically about the role and influence of media in society.

Students studying Media Studies at GCSE level will need knowledge of the following:

Media Language: This topic covers the various techniques used in media texts such as camera angles, lighting, sound, editing, and mise-en-scene. Understanding how these techniques are used can help students analyze media texts and develop their own media products.

Audience: Understanding the target audience is crucial when it comes to creating media products. Students should be familiar with different audience demographics, such as age, gender, socio-economic status, and culture, and how these factors influence media consumption.

Representation: This topic focuses on the ways in which different social groups are represented in media texts. It's important for students to understand how media can shape people's perceptions of different groups and the impact this can have on society.

Industry: The media industry is vast and complex, and students should be familiar with its key players, including media conglomerates, production companies, and advertising agencies. Understanding the economics of media is also important, as it can impact the types of media products that are produced and consumed.

Media Forms: GCSE Media covers a range of media forms, including film, television, advertising, print media, and online media. Students should be familiar with the characteristics of each form and how they differ from one another.

Media Institutions: This topic covers the various institutions that shape media production and consumption, including regulatory bodies, such as Ofcom and the BBFC, and media watchdogs, such as the Media Standards Trust.

Social Media: Social media has become an increasingly important part of our lives, and students should be familiar with the various platforms and their impact on society. Topics such as fake news, social media addiction, and online privacy are all important considerations when studying social media.

So let's begin our revision with the most important, that is to understand media terms, their meaning and where they are used.

Terms, their meaning and application in Media Studies

The Media Industry

The media industry refers to the collection of businesses and organizations that create, distribute, and monetize content for mass audiences. This includes a wide range of sectors such as television, radio, film, publishing, advertising, music, video games, social media, and digital media. The media industry encompasses various roles, from content creators such as writers, journalists, and producers to technicians and engineers responsible for distribution and broadcasting. It is a rapidly evolving and growing industry that plays a significant role in shaping public opinion, culture, and entertainment, and has a considerable impact on the global economy.

Traditional Media

Traditional media refers to forms of communication and entertainment that existed before the advent of the internet and digital technology. These forms of media include print media, such as newspapers, magazines, and books, as well as broadcast media, such as radio and television. Traditional media channels are typically mass media, with a one-way flow of information from the producer to the consumer. They are typically more expensive to produce and have a limited reach compared to digital media, but are often regarded as more credible and trustworthy. While digital media has become increasingly popular, traditional media continues to play an important role in shaping public opinion and providing a source of news and entertainment.

Media Convergence

Media convergence refers to the merging of various forms of media content, technologies, and platforms into a single unified system. It is the process by which different types of media, such as print, broadcast, and digital, are combined to create new forms of communication and entertainment. Media convergence has been facilitated by technological advancements, such as the internet, social media, and mobile devices, which have made it possible for people to access and interact with various types of media content in new and innovative ways. Examples of media convergence include the use of multimedia content on websites, the integration of television with the internet, and the convergence of mobile devices, (such as smart phones and tablets,) with traditional media forms.

Media convergence has had a significant impact on the media industry, changing the way content is produced, distributed, and consumed, and creating new opportunities for media companies to reach audiences.

The Media Industry

The media industry is a business that is focused on the creation, production, and distribution of media content for profit. The industry includes a wide range of companies, from small independent studios to large multinational corporations, which operate across various media sectors, such as film, television, publishing, advertising, music, and digital media.

These companies invest significant resources in the development of media content, from research and development to production and marketing, with the ultimate goal of generating revenue and maximizing profits.

Media companies employ various business models, such as advertising-supported, subscription-based, or pay-per-view, to monetize their content and generate revenue. The media industry is highly competitive, with companies vying for audience attention and market share, and is constantly evolving to keep pace with changes in technology and consumer preferences.

Media Industry marketing and promotion

Marketing and promotion are essential components of the media industry. Media companies invest significant resources in advertising and promoting their products to reach and engage audiences. Marketing and promotion activities help media companies to create brand awareness, generate interest in their products, and increase sales.

Marketing activities in the media industry may include traditional forms of advertising, such as print ads, billboards, and television commercials. However, with the rise of digital media, many media companies have shifted their marketing efforts to online channels, such as social media, email marketing, and online advertising.

Promotion in the media industry may involve partnering with other brands or media outlets to increase visibility and exposure. For example, a movie studio may partner with a fast-food chain to offer promotional merchandise, such as toys, to increase interest in the movie among children.

Media companies also use public relations (PR) strategies to manage their image and reputation. PR activities may include issuing press releases, organizing media events, and engaging with influencers and journalists.

Overall, marketing and promotion activities in the media industry are critical to the success of media products and the growth of media companies. By investing in effective marketing and promotion strategies, media companies can generate excitement and interest in their products and attract and retain a loyal audience.

Television

Television (TV) is a widely used form of media that provides visual and auditory entertainment and information to audiences in their homes. It consists of broadcast programming, which is transmitted over the airwaves to a receiver, and cable or satellite programming, which is then delivered via a wired or wireless network. TV programming includes news, drama, comedy, documentaries, sports, and reality shows, among other genres.

TV has been a dominant medium for several decades, providing a shared cultural experience for families and communities. It is also an influential platform for shaping public opinion and political discourse. The TV industry has undergone significant changes in recent years, as audiences have shifted away from traditional TV programming to streaming services and on-demand viewing. However, TV remains a significant source of entertainment and information for millions of people worldwide.

The TV industry is highly competitive, with networks and studios vying for audience attention and advertising revenue. Major TV networks, such as ABC, NBC, CBS, and Fox, produce and distribute programming across the United States, while cable and satellite providers, such as HBO and Showtime, produce original programming and offer on-demand access to popular TV shows and movies. In the United Kingdom, we have the BBC, ITV and Channel 4. Other cable and satellite providers include Prime, Netflix and Sky. (There are many more than these)

TV production involves a complex process, from ideation and scriptwriting to filming and post-production. A typical TV production team may include writers, directors, producers, actors, cinematographers, editors, and sound technicians. The TV industry also employs a large number of support staff, such as marketing and advertising professionals, lawyers, and accountants.

Overall, TV continues to be an important part of the media landscape, providing entertainment, information, and social connection to audiences worldwide.

TV innovation

The television (TV) industry has seen significant innovation and evolution in recent years, with the development of new technologies and the changing habits of audiences. Some notable TV innovations include:

High-Definition (HD) and Ultra High-Definition (UHD) - HD and UHD technology offer higher quality video and audio, with more vibrant colours, greater clarity, and sharper detail. This has become the new standard for TV programming, as well as for home video and streaming services.

Streaming and on-demand services - The rise of streaming services, such as Netflix, Hulu, and Amazon Prime, has changed the way audiences consume TV programming. These services offer on-demand access to entire series, with the ability to binge-watch multiple episodes in one sitting.

Smart TVs - Smart TVs integrate internet and app-based features directly into the TV itself, allowing users to access streaming services, social media, and web browsing without the need for a separate device.

Second-screen viewing - Second-screen viewing involves using a mobile device, such as a smart phone or tablet, to enhance the TV-watching experience. Viewers can use second screens to access program information, engage with social media, and even interact with the TV show in real-time.

Virtual and Augmented Reality - Virtual and augmented reality technology is beginning to make its way into the TV industry, offering immersive experiences for viewers. This technology can create 3D environments, interactive elements, and new ways of storytelling.

Overall, the TV industry has seen significant innovation and evolution in recent years, with new technologies and changing audience habits driving new trends and opportunities.

TV Content

At GCSE Media level, TV content refers to the programs, films, and advertisements broadcast on television. TV content is created by production companies and studios, who develop ideas and commission writers, directors, actors, and other production staff to create the final product.

GCSE Media students must study TV content in detail, analyzing its form, structure, and content. You as a student will explore how TV programs are constructed to appeal to specific audiences, using narrative, camera techniques, editing, sound, and other production elements to create meaning and engage viewers.

As a GCSE Media student, you also need to be able to analyze TV content in terms of genre, considering the conventions and expectations of specific genres, such as drama, comedy, and reality TV. You will need to be able to examine how TV content reflects and influences cultural values and social issues, exploring the messages and themes conveyed through TV programming.

In addition to analyzing TV content, you may also be required to create your own TV content, such as short films, news segments, or advertisements. This involves developing ideas, planning and pre-production, filming and post-production, and evaluating the final product. (Please check your individual syllabus and curriculum of your examination body for details)

Overall, the study of TV content is an important aspect of GCSE Media, as it provides students with a deeper understanding of the TV industry, the creative process of producing TV content, and the role of TV in shaping cultural values and social issues.

Genre and Subgenres

In media studies, genre refers to a category or type of content, characterized by specific conventions, themes, and styles. Genres help audiences understand what to expect from a particular type of media, such as a film, TV show, or book, and can be a useful tool for creators in shaping their content to meet audience expectations. Here are some examples of genres and their subgenres:

Film Genres:

Action: subgenres include martial arts, western, and superhero films

Comedy: subgenres include romantic comedy, slapstick comedy, and parody films

Drama: subgenres include historical drama, biographical drama, and melodrama

Horror: subgenres include slasher films, supernatural horror, and psychological horror

Science Fiction: subgenres include space opera, dystopian, and time travel films

Television Genres:

Drama: subgenres include crime drama, medical drama, and legal drama

Reality TV: subgenres include competition shows, makeover shows, and docuseries

Comedy: subgenres include sitcoms, sketch comedy, and dark comedy

News and Current Affairs: subgenres include local news, national news, and investigative journalism

Sports: subgenres include live events, news and analysis, and documentaries

Literary Genres:

Fiction: subgenres include romance, mystery, and science fiction

Nonfiction: subgenres include memoirs, biographies, and self-help books

Poetry: subgenres include sonnets, haikus, and free verse

Drama: subgenres include tragedy, comedy, and historical drama

Fantasy: subgenres include high fantasy, urban fantasy, and fairy tales

Overall, genres and subgenres help to categorize and define different types of media, making it easier for audiences and creators to communicate and engage with each other.

Scheduling choices

Scheduling choices in the media industry refer to the decisions made by broadcasters and other media outlets about when to air or publish specific content, such as TV shows, films, or articles. These choices can have a significant impact on audience engagement and the success of a particular piece of content. Some common scheduling choices include:

Prime Time: This refers to the period of the day or week when the largest number of viewers are available to watch television. In most countries, prime time is between 7:00 PM and 10:00 PM on weekdays, and slightly earlier on weekends. Broadcasting content during this period is generally considered more valuable, as it has the potential to attract a larger audience and generate higher advertising revenue.

Sweeps: Television sweeps periods are specific periods during the year when broadcasters measure their viewership ratings in order to set advertising rates. Sweeps periods typically occur in February, May, July, and November, and as a result, broadcasters may schedule high-profile or special programming during these times to attract more viewers and increase their ratings.

Counterprogramming: Counterprogramming involves scheduling content that is designed to appeal to a different audience than that of competing networks or outlets, with the aim of attracting viewers away from other programs. For example, a network might schedule a romantic comedy movie to air opposite a high-profile sporting event, in the hope of drawing a different demographic of viewers.

On-Demand and Streaming Services: With the rise of on-demand and streaming services, such as Netflix and Amazon Prime, scheduling choices have become less important in terms of determining audience engagement. These services allow viewers to watch content at any time, on any device, meaning that audiences have more control over when and how they engage with media.

Overall, scheduling choices are an important aspect of the media industry, as they can have a significant impact on audience engagement and the success of specific content. Understanding scheduling strategies is crucial for media professionals, as they seek to maximize the reach and impact of their programming.

Media Techniques

Media Companies use a number of techniques to achieve their goals. The following are those you need to know for your GCSE Media Examination.

Stripping is a media scheduling technique that involves broadcasting the same TV show or program at the same time every day or every week, typically at a time when a large number of viewers are available to watch. The goal of stripping is to build a loyal audience by providing viewers with a reliable and predictable viewing experience.

This technique is commonly used for daytime TV programs, such as soap operas, talk shows, and game shows, as well as for prime-time news and entertainment shows. Stripping helps to build a regular viewing habit among audiences, and can also be used to help promote other shows or events by airing promos or advertisements during the program.

Stripping is just one of many techniques used in media to maximize audience engagement and build a loyal following.

Other Techniques

Other techniques may include cliff-hangers, teasers, cross-promotion, and exclusives, among others. Each technique is designed to engage audiences in a different way, and media professionals will choose the techniques that best suit their content and audience to achieve their goals.

Defensive, offensive, hammocking, and pre-echo are also all media scheduling techniques that can be used to optimize the success of specific programming. Here's a brief explanation of each:

Defensive scheduling: This is a technique used by broadcasters to protect their audience from competitors' programming. For example, if one network has a popular show that is being threatened by a competing show airing at the same time, the network may choose to schedule a different program that caters to a similar audience, effectively "defending" their audience from switching to the competitor.

Offensive scheduling: This technique involves scheduling a popular program against a weaker or less popular competing program, in order to "attack" the competitor and draw viewers away from that program. This technique is often used to directly compete against a program that is airing at the same time on a different network or channel.

Hammocking: This technique involves scheduling a new or untested program between two established programs in order to give the new program a better chance of success. The idea is that viewers will be more likely to tune in to the new program if it is surrounded by established programs that they already enjoy.

Pre-echo: This technique involves airing a teaser or trailer for an upcoming program before the current program has ended, in order to generate interest and anticipation for the new program. This technique is often used for high-profile programs or events, such as season finales or awards shows.

Each of these scheduling techniques can be used to promote a program, protect an audience, or directly compete against other networks or channels. Media professionals must carefully consider the goals and audience of their programming in order to choose the scheduling technique that is best suited to their needs.

Zoning

Zoning in media studies refers to the process of dividing a city or region into different areas, or "zones," for the purpose of regulating the use and distribution of media content. This can include restrictions on the types of media that can be broadcast or distributed in a particular zone, as well as regulations on the placement and size of media infrastructure, such as billboards and television antennas. Zoning can have significant impacts on the media landscape and the way that media content is consumed and distributed within a given region.

Inheritance

In media studies, inheritance refers to the ways in which cultural values, beliefs, and practices are passed down from one generation to the next through various forms of media, such as books, films, television shows, and social media. It is the process by which cultural knowledge and traditions are preserved and transmitted across time and space. Inheritance can also refer to the ways in which media texts and genres build upon and reference earlier works and styles, and how audiences interpret and respond to these references.

In this sense, media inheritance can have significant impacts on cultural memory and identity, as well as on the development of media industries and aesthetics over time.

Television studios and their marketing

Television studios use a variety of marketing strategies to promote themselves and their programs, including:

Trailers and Teasers: They release trailers and teasers of upcoming shows, seasons or episodes to create buzz and generate interest among their target audience.

Social Media: They utilize social media platforms to connect with fans and build communities around their shows. They also create and share engaging content, such as behind-the-scenes footage, interviews with cast and crew, and interactive games and quizzes.

Publicity and Press: They arrange press releases and publicity events, such as red carpet premieres, to generate media coverage and promote their shows.

Collaborations and Partnerships: They collaborate with other brands and organizations to cross-promote their shows and reach new audiences. For example, a TV studio may partner with a streaming service or a product company to promote their show and offer special promotions.

Merchandising: They develop and sell merchandise related to their shows, such as t-shirts, mugs, and other products, to create additional revenue streams and promote brand awareness.

Awards and Festivals: They participate in industry awards and festivals to showcase their work and promote their shows to industry professionals and potential partners.

Television studios employ a mix of traditional and modern marketing techniques to reach their target audience and build brand recognition.

Sample Case Studies

A case study is an in-depth research method used to analyze a particular individual, group and to gain insights into its characteristics, behaviours, and outcomes. The case study method involves collecting and analyzing a range of data from various sources, such as interviews, surveys, observations, and documents, to create a detailed and comprehensive picture of the subject being studied.

Case studies can be used in a variety of fields, including business, psychology, sociology, medicine, and education. For example, in a business context, a case study may focus on a specific company or organization, and examine its operations, strategy, and performance over a period of time. The case study may explore challenges the company has faced, and the decisions it has taken.

An example case studies of TV marketing

A case study of TV marketing in the television industry may involve an in-depth analysis of a particular TV show or network's marketing strategy and its impact on the show's success. For example, a case study could examine the marketing campaign for the hit television series "Game of Thrones" and how it contributed to the show's popularity and longevity.

The case study may examine various elements of the marketing campaign, such as the show's trailers and teasers, social media presence, publicity events, collaborations and partnerships, and merchandising efforts. It may also explore the target audience for the show and how the marketing campaign effectively reached and engaged that audience.

The case study may use a range of data sources to gain insights into the effectiveness of the marketing campaign, including audience viewership data, social media analytics, and sales data for merchandise related to the show. The study may also analyze the broader cultural and industry context in which the show was marketed, such as trends in TV consumption and competition from other shows and networks.

The case study could provide valuable insights into the strategies and tactics used by TV networks to market their shows and reach audiences in an increasingly competitive media landscape. It could also highlight the role of marketing in the success of TV shows and the broader television industry.

Example 2 - A TV Marketing Case Study

Another case study in TV marketing could be a detailed analysis of the marketing campaign for the streaming service Disney+, and how it contributed to the platform's rapid growth and success.

The case study may examine the various elements of Disney's marketing campaign, including its advertising efforts, social media presence, public relations events, content partnerships, and brand positioning. The study may also explore how the marketing campaign targeted different audiences, such as families, children, and fans of specific franchises like Star Wars and Marvel.

The case study may use a range of data sources to gain insights into the effectiveness of the marketing campaign, such as subscriber numbers, audience demographics, social media engagement, and customer satisfaction surveys. The study may also analyze the broader market and competitive landscape, such as trends in streaming media consumption and competition from other streaming services like Netflix and Amazon Prime Video.

The case study could provide valuable insights into the strategies and tactics used by Disney+ to build its brand and attract subscribers, as well as the broader trends and challenges in the streaming media industry. It could also highlight the importance of effective marketing in the success of new media platforms and the broader media landscape.

Television programmes as media texts

Television programmes are media texts. This means they are cultural products that communicate meaning and values through visual and audio elements. As media texts, television programmes are constructed and distributed by media industries, and consumed and interpreted by audiences.

Television programmes as media texts can be analyzed through various frameworks, such as textual analysis, reception analysis, and political economy.

Textual analysis examines the formal elements of a television programme, such as its narrative structure, cinematography, editing, and sound design, to identify patterns and meanings embedded within the text. For example, a textual analysis of a TV drama may explore how camera angles and lighting are used to create a sense of suspense or drama.

Reception analysis, on the other hand, focuses on how audiences receive and interpret television programmes, and how these interpretations are influenced by factors such as social context, cultural background, and personal experiences. Reception analysis may involve conducting surveys, interviews, or focus groups to gather data on how viewers understand and respond to television programmes.

Political economy analysis, examines the economic and institutional factors that shape the production and distribution of television programmes. For example, a political economy analysis may investigate how ownership structures and revenue models affect the types of programmes produced and the ways they are distributed.

Overall, analyzing television programmes as media texts allows us to better understand the cultural and social meanings embedded within them, as well as the ways they are created, consumed, and circulated in the broader media landscape.

TV regulations and how they work:

TV regulations refer to the legal and institutional frameworks that govern the creation, distribution, and consumption of television content. These regulations are put in place to ensure that television content adheres to certain standards and serves the public interest.

TV regulations can vary by country, but they typically cover a range of areas, such as content, advertising, ownership, and access. Some common examples of TV regulations include:

Content regulations: These regulations may set standards for what can and cannot be shown on television, such as restrictions on violence, nudity, and offensive language. They may also require certain types of programming, such as news or educational content, to be included in TV schedules.

Advertising regulations: These regulations may limit the amount and types of advertising that can be shown on TV, such as restrictions on advertising to children or advertising for certain products like tobacco or alcohol.

Ownership regulations: These regulations may restrict the ownership and control of TV stations and networks, to prevent monopolies and ensure diversity of voices in the media landscape.

Access regulations: These regulations may require TV stations to provide closed captioning, audio description, or sign language interpretation for people with disabilities. They may also require TV stations to provide local content or programming in certain languages to serve minority or marginalized communities.

TV regulations are typically enforced by government agencies, such as the Federal Communications Commission in the United States, and violations can result in fines, license revocation, or other penalties. Overall, TV regulations play an important role in shaping the content and accessibility of television, and ensuring that it serves the public interest.

Watershed in Television Broadcasting

In television broadcasting, a watershed refers to a specific time of day, usually in the evening, after which broadcasters are allowed to air programs with more mature or adult content. This time is typically set by the regulatory body that oversees television broadcasting in a particular country, and it may vary from country to country.

In the United Kingdom, for example, the watershed is set at 9:00 pm and indicates a point in the evening after which broadcasters can show content with more mature themes, such as violence, sex, and drug use.

Before the watershed, broadcasters are expected to air programs that are suitable for a general audience, such as family-friendly shows and news programs.

The purpose of the watershed is to protect children and young people from exposure to inappropriate content, while still allowing adults to watch and enjoy more mature content after a certain time of day. Broadcasters are expected to adhere to the watershed rules and to air appropriate content during different times of the day.

In some countries, the watershed is not a formal regulation but is instead a guideline for broadcasters to follow. In these cases, the responsibility for monitoring and enforcing content guidelines may fall on the broadcaster or an independent regulatory body.

The watershed is an important concept in television broadcasting that helps to ensure that content is appropriate for different audiences and that children and young people are protected from exposure to inappropriate material.

Magazines

Magazines are publications that are typically produced on a regular basis, such as weekly, monthly, or quarterly. They are usually printed on glossy paper and contain a mix of articles, photographs, and illustrations on a specific topic or variety of topics.

Magazines cover a wide range of subjects, from fashion and beauty to sports, news, politics, entertainment, technology, and more. They are often targeted at specific demographics, such as women, men, teens, or seniors, and may have a particular focus on a particular geographic region or cultural group.

Magazines are often available for purchase at newsstands, bookstores, and other retail outlets. They may also be available by subscription, which typically provides readers with a lower cost per issue and the convenience of having the magazine delivered directly to their mailbox.

Magazines are a popular form of entertainment and information for many people, and they can offer in-depth reporting, analysis, and commentary on a variety of topics. They can also provide a platform for writers, photographers, and other creatives to showcase their work and build a following.

The following are some examples of popular magazines and their subgenres:

Time Magazine - A weekly news magazine covering a broad range of topics from politics and culture to technology and science.

Vogue - A monthly fashion and lifestyle magazine that covers the latest trends in fashion, beauty, and culture.

Sports Illustrated - A weekly sports magazine that covers professional and amateur sports, including football, basketball, baseball, and more.

National Geographic - A monthly magazine that explores science, history, geography, and culture through stunning photography and in-depth reporting.

People - A weekly celebrity and human-interest magazine that covers entertainment news, celebrity gossip, and human-interest stories.

Forbes - A biweekly business magazine that focuses on finance, entrepreneurship, and wealth management.

Cosmopolitan - A monthly magazine for young women that covers fashion, beauty, health, relationships, and sex.

Wired - A monthly technology magazine that covers the latest trends in technology, including gadgets, software, and internet culture.

The Economist - A weekly news magazine that covers global politics, economics, and business.

Rolling Stone - A monthly music and popular culture magazine that covers music news, album reviews, and artist profiles.

These are just a few examples of the many magazines that exist in various subgenres. Other subgenres include food and cooking, travel, home and garden, science fiction and fantasy, and many more.

Publishers of these magazines

The names of the publishers of some of the magazines mentioned above are as follows:

Time Magazine - Time USA, LLC

Vogue - Condé Nast

Sports Illustrated - Maven Coalition, LLC

National Geographic - National Geographic Partners, LLC

People - Meredith Corporation

Forbes - Forbes Media LLC

Cosmopolitan - Hearst Communications, Inc.

Wired - Condé Nast

The Economist - The Economist Group

Rolling Stone - Penske Media Corporation

It's worth noting that some magazines may have different publishers depending on the region or country in which they are published. For example Vogue America has a different publisher to Vogue UK.

Please do your own research to collate the information you may need regarding this.

Factors that determine a successful magazine

There are several factors that can contribute to the success of a magazine, including:

Strong and consistent editorial content: A successful magazine should have high-quality content that is relevant, informative, and engaging to its target audience. The magazine should provide a unique perspective or voice that differentiates it from other publications.

A clear and focused target audience: A successful magazine should have a clear understanding of its target audience and cater to their interests and needs. By knowing who their audience is, the magazine can create content and marketing campaigns that resonate with them.

Effective distribution and promotion: A successful magazine should be distributed through multiple channels, including news-stands, subscriptions, and online. Additionally, the magazine should have effective marketing and promotion campaigns that reach and attract its target audience.

High-quality design and visual elements: A successful magazine should have visually appealing design, photography, and illustrations that enhance its content and engage its readers. A consistent and recognizable visual brand can help build the magazine's reputation and attract new readers.

Strong relationships with advertisers: A successful magazine should have strong relationships with advertisers and provide them with effective and creative advertising solutions. Advertisers can provide a significant source of revenue for the magazine and help support its ongoing success.

Adaptability and innovation: A successful magazine should be adaptable and open to change, especially as technology and readers' interests evolve. The magazine should continually innovate and experiment with new formats, platforms, and content to stay relevant and meet readers' needs.

Overall, a successful magazine is one that provides high-quality content, effectively reaches its target audience, and is financially sustainable.

How to Analyse a Magazine

Here are some steps to help you analyse a magazine:

Identify the magazine's target audience: Look at the magazine's content, advertisements, and visual design to determine who the magazine is targeting. Consider age, gender, interests, and other demographic factors.

Analyze the editorial content: Look at the types of articles and features in the magazine, their quality, tone, and relevance to the target audience. Consider the writing style, author's credentials, and whether the content is fact-based or opinionated.

Analyze the magazine's visual elements: Look at the magazine's layout, typography, photography, and illustrations. Consider how these elements contribute to the magazine's visual appeal and effectiveness in conveying its content.

Evaluate the quality of the magazine's production: Consider the quality of the paper, print, and binding of the magazine. Look for any flaws or errors in the production, as this may indicate a lack of attention to detail or quality.

Analyze the advertising: Look at the advertisements in the magazine and consider how they are targeted to the magazine's audience. Consider the quality and effectiveness of the advertising, as well as the balance between advertising and editorial content.

Evaluate the magazine's overall design and branding: Consider the magazine's overall visual identity and how it aligns with the target audience and content. Look at the consistency of the design across issues, as well as any changes over time.

Consider the magazine's impact and success: Look at the magazine's circulation, readership, and reputation in the industry. Consider any awards or recognition the magazine has received, as well as any criticisms or controversies.

The above steps can help you gain a better understanding of a magazine's content, audience, and overall quality, which can help you evaluate its effectiveness and relevance to your interests or needs.

The decline of the magazine industry

The magazine industry has been facing a decline in recent years due to a number of factors, including:

The rise of digital media: The popularity of digital media, including online news and social media, has led to a decline in print magazine readership. Many readers now prefer to consume news and information online, which has resulted in declining magazine sales and subscriptions.

Competition from free content: The availability of free content on the internet has made it more difficult for magazines to compete. Readers can access a wealth of information online, which has made them less likely to pay for print magazines.

Advertisers shifting their budgets to digital: Advertisers are increasingly shifting their advertising budgets to digital media, including social media and online advertising. This has led to a decline in print magazine advertising revenue.

Changes in consumer Behaviour: Consumer Behaviour has changed over the years, with many people now preferring to consume content on-the-go and in smaller, bite-sized formats. This has made it more challenging for print magazines to maintain readership.

Economic downturns: Economic downturns and recessions can also impact the magazine industry. When people have less disposable income, they may be less likely to spend money on print magazines.

These factors have led to a decline in the magazine industry, with many print publications struggling to stay afloat. Many magazines have had to reduce their print runs or switch to digital formats in order to survive. However, some publications have been able to adapt to the changing landscape by focusing on niche topics or offering high-quality, specialized content that is not easily found online.

Podcasts

Podcasts have experienced a surge in popularity in recent years, with more and more people tuning in to listen to their favourite shows. There are several reasons for the rise of podcasts, including:

Convenience: Podcasts are convenient to listen to, as they can be streamed or downloaded and listened to on-the-go, while exercising, or while commuting. This flexibility has made it easier for people to consume content on their own terms.

Diverse content: Podcasts cover a wide range of topics and genres, from news and politics to entertainment, sports, and personal development. There is something for everyone, and listeners can easily find shows that cater to their interests and needs.

Low barrier to entry: Starting a podcast is relatively easy and inexpensive, which has led to a proliferation of new shows. This has created a diverse and vibrant podcast community that continues to grow.

Intimacy and engagement: Podcasts offer a unique level of intimacy and engagement, as listeners can connect with the hosts and guests on a personal level. The conversational format of many podcasts creates a sense of community and connection that is hard to replicate in other media.

Revenue opportunities: Podcasts offer a range of revenue opportunities, including advertising, sponsorships, and merchandise sales. As more listeners tune in, podcasters have been able to monetize their shows and turn them into profitable businesses.

Podcasts have now become a popular and engaging form of media, with a diverse range of content and a growing community of listeners and creators.

Advertising in Media Studies

Advertising is a central topic in media studies, as it plays a critical role in the media industry and influences the way that media is produced, distributed, and consumed. Here are some key aspects of advertising in G.C.S.E. Media Studies:

Purpose and function: Advertising is a form of communication that is designed to promote and sell products, services, or ideas to a target audience. It is a key revenue source for many media companies, including print, broadcast, and online media.

Forms and strategies: Advertising takes many forms, including print ads, radio and TV commercials, online ads, and social media campaigns. It uses various strategies to grab attention, persuade, and influence consumers, including emotional appeals, humour, celebrity endorsements, and appeals to social status.

Cultural and social implications: Advertising is not just a commercial enterprise but also has cultural and social implications. It influences how people perceive themselves, their needs and desires, and their relationship to the world around them. Advertising can reinforce existing cultural norms or challenge them, and it can create new trends and fashions.

Ethics and regulation: Advertising raises ethical issues around truthfulness, accuracy, and manipulation. Many countries have regulations that govern advertising to ensure that it is not misleading, offensive, or harmful. However, enforcing these regulations can be difficult, and advertising can still have negative effects on vulnerable audiences, such as children and the elderly.

Future of advertising: The media landscape is changing rapidly, and so is the advertising industry. New technologies, such as artificial intelligence and augmented reality, are creating new opportunities and challenges for advertisers. The rise of social media and user-generated content is also changing the way that brands and consumers interact, creating new forms of advertising that blur the line between commercial and non-commercial content.

You should note that advertising is a complex and multifaceted topic in media studies, and it is important to consider its various dimensions when analyzing the role of media in society. It can be found on a wide range of media platforms, including the following:

Television: Ads are a common feature on television, where they are shown during commercial breaks between programs. TV ads can be targeted to specific demographics, such as age, gender, or location, and can be highly effective in reaching large audiences.

Print: Ads can also be found in print media, including newspapers, magazines, and billboards. Print ads can be highly targeted to specific audiences and can be an effective way to reach consumers in a particular region or niche market.

Online: The internet has revolutionized advertising, and ads can now be found on a wide range of online platforms, including search engines, social media, and mobile apps. Online ads can be highly targeted based on user data, such as search history, location, and interests, and can be customized to different formats, such as display ads, search ads, and native ads.

Radio: Ads can also be found on radio stations, where they are typically played between songs or during commercial breaks. Radio ads can be highly targeted based on geographic location and demographic data.

Out-of-home: Ads can be found in public places, such as billboards, bus shelters, and transit stations. Out-of-home ads can be highly effective in reaching consumers while they are on-the-go, and can be customized to different formats, such as static billboards, digital billboards, and interactive installations.

Events: Ads can be found at events, such as concerts, sports games, and festivals. Event-based ads can be highly effective in reaching large, engaged audiences and can be customized to different formats, such as banners, billboards, and branded installations.

So to recap: Advertising can be found on a wide range of media platforms, and the choice of platform depends on the target audience, the advertising budget, and the advertising goals.

Advertising Techniques

There are many different techniques used in advertising, and advertisers often use a combination of techniques to create effective campaigns. Below are some common techniques used in campaigns with examples:

Emotional appeals: Ads that use emotional appeals aim to evoke feelings of joy, sadness, anger, or fear to create a connection with the audience. Examples include the "Lost Dog" commercial from Budweiser, which uses a cute puppy to evoke feelings of joy and connection with the brand.

Humour: Ads that use humour aim to make the audience laugh and create a positive association with the brand. Examples include the Geico "Hump Day" commercial, which uses a talking camel to create a humourous and memorable ad.

Celebrity endorsements: Ads that use celebrity endorsements aim to leverage the popularity and credibility of celebrities to promote a product or service. Examples include Michael Jordan's endorsement of Nike, which helped establish the brand as a leader in the athletic shoe market.

Bandwagon: Ads that use bandwagon techniques aim to create a sense of social proof by implying that everyone is using or buying a particular product or service. Examples include Apple's "Get a Mac" campaign, which implied that everyone was switching to Apple computers.

Product demonstration: Ads that use product demonstration techniques aim to show the benefits or features of a product in action. Examples include the "Will It Blend?" campaign from Blendtec, which demonstrated the power of its blenders by blending a variety of unusual objects.

Fear appeals: Ads that use fear appeals aim to create a sense of urgency or concern to motivate the audience to take action. Examples include antismoking ads that use graphic images to show the health consequences of smoking.

Testimonials: Ads that use testimonials aim to use the positive experiences of real people to create a positive association with the brand. Examples include the "Subway Sandwich Challenge" campaign, which used testimonials from real people who lost weight by eating Subway sandwiches.

Nostalgia: Ads that use nostalgia aim to evoke positive memories and emotions from the past. Examples include Coca-Cola's "Share a Coke" campaign, which personalized its bottles with people's names to tap into nostalgic feelings.

Sex appeal: Ads that use sex appeal aim to create a sense of desire and attraction to the product or service being advertised. Examples include Calvin Klein's fragrance ads, which often feature scantily clad models to create a sense of sexiness and luxury.

Storytelling: Ads that use storytelling aim to create a narrative around the product or service being advertised. Examples include Google's "Year in Search" ads, which use real stories and events to highlight the power of search and connection.

Shock value: Ads that use shock value aim to create a sense of surprise or shock to grab the audience's attention. Examples include PETA's controversial ads, which use graphic images and shocking statements to promote animal rights.

Value proposition: Ads that use value proposition aim to show the unique benefits and advantages of a product or service over the competition. Examples include the "Priceless" campaign from Mastercard, which emphasized the value of experiences over material possessions.

Online and Social Media Advertising Techniques

There are many different internet advertising techniques, and the most effective ones will depend on the business and its target audience.
Some of the most common internet advertising techniques are as follows:

Display ads: Display ads are visual ads that appear on websites, typically in the form of banner ads or sidebar ads. They can be targeted to specific audiences based on factors such as location, interests, and browsing history.

Search engine marketing: Search engine marketing (SEM) involves placing ads on search engine results pages. These ads appear above or alongside organic search results and are triggered by specific search terms.

Social media advertising: Social media advertising involves placing ads on social media platforms such as Facebook, Instagram, Twitter, and LinkedIn. These ads can be highly targeted based on factors such as age, gender, interests, and location.

Influencer marketing: Influencer marketing involves partnering with social media influencers to promote your brand or product. Influencers typically have large followings on social media and can be effective in reaching specific target audiences.

Video advertising: Video advertising involves placing ads in online videos, such as those on YouTube or other video-sharing platforms. These ads can be skippable or non-skippable and can be targeted based on factors such as location, interests, and demographics.

Retargeting: Retargeting involves targeting ads to people who have previously visited your website or interacted with your brand online. This technique can be effective in keeping your brand top of mind and encouraging people to return to your website. Companies like Amazon use this technique.

Native advertising: Native advertising involves placing ads that match the look and feel of the content on a website. These ads are designed to be less disruptive than traditional ads and can be effective in engaging audiences.

Programmatic advertising: Programmatic advertising involves using software to automate the buying and selling of digital ads. This technique can be highly targeted and can help optimize ad performance.

Email marketing: Email marketing involves sending promotional messages to a targeted audience via email. This technique can be highly effective in building customer relationships and driving sales.

Affiliate marketing: Affiliate marketing involves partnering with other businesses or individuals to promote your brand or product. Affiliates receive a commission for any sales that result from their promotional efforts.

Mobile advertising: Mobile advertising involves placing ads on mobile devices, such as smart phones and tablets. This technique can be highly effective in reaching audiences on the go.

Geofencing: Geofencing involves targeting ads to people within a specific geographic location, such as a particular city or neighbourhood. This technique can be effective in promoting local businesses and events.

The cost of Advertising

Advertising costs can range from a few hundred Pound Sterling for a small campaign to millions of Pounds for a large, high-profile campaign. It's important that businesses carefully consider their advertising goals and budget and work with a reputable advertising agency or media buyer to develop a cost-effective and impactful advertising strategy which works well for their business.

You should note that advertisers, manufacturers and producers may use a combination of techniques to create effective campaigns that connect with their target audience and achieve their advertising goals. However, doubling up on techniques or using more than one this has a tendency to increase advertising cost which can vary widely depending on many different factors, including the platform or medium used, the type of ad, the target audience, the duration and frequency of the campaign, and the level of competition in the market.

A general consideration that advertisers keep in mind when deciding about what advertising technique to use aside of their target is to think about advertising costs which can greatly differ depending on a number of factors. Below are factors that influence and affect the cost of advertising:

Platform or medium: Different advertising platforms, such as television, radio, print, digital, or outdoor advertising, have different costs associated with them. For example, a 30-second commercial during the Super Bowl can cost millions of dollars, while a social media ad may only cost a few dollars per click.

Type of ad: The type of ad being used can also affect the cost. For example, a full-page print ad in a popular magazine may be more expensive than a small classified ad.

Target audience: The cost of advertising may also depend on the target audience. For example, if you're trying to reach a very niche audience, such as luxury car buyers or avid hikers, it may cost more to reach them through targeted advertising.

Duration and frequency: The length and frequency of the campaign can also affect the cost. Longer campaigns or more frequent ads may cost more than shorter or less frequent campaigns.

Competition: The level of competition in the market can also affect the cost of advertising. If there are many other businesses competing for the same audience, the cost of advertising may be higher to stand out.

Regulation with regards to advertising

There are various regulations governing advertising, and these regulations can vary depending on the country or region. Here are a few examples of regulations that may apply to advertising in the UK:

Truth in advertising: Advertisers must not make false or misleading claims in their advertisements. This includes claims about the quality or performance of a product, as well as claims about pricing or discounts.

Advertising to children: Advertising aimed at children is subject to additional regulations to protect minors from potentially harmful or inappropriate content. These regulations may include restrictions on the use of certain types of advertising, such as ads for alcohol or tobacco.

Privacy and data protection: Advertisers must comply with regulations governing the collection and use of personal data for advertising purposes. This may include obtaining consent from individuals before collecting or using their data, and providing clear information about how their data will be used.

Intellectual property: Advertisers must not infringe on the intellectual property rights of others in their advertising. This may include using copyrighted material without permission or using trademarks in a way that implies endorsement or association with a product or service.

Advertising in specific industries: Certain industries, such as healthcare and financial services, may be subject to additional regulations governing advertising to protect consumers and ensure ethical practices.

Comparative advertising: Comparative advertising, which involves making comparisons between two or more products, may be subject to additional regulations to ensure that the comparisons are fair and accurate.

Endorsements and testimonials: Advertisers must be transparent about any endorsements or testimonials used in their ads. This may include disclosing any financial or other incentives provided to the endorser, and ensuring that the endorsement accurately reflects the endorser's experience with the product or service.

Environmental claims: Advertisers must be careful when making claims about the environmental impact of their products or services. Claims must be truthful and accurate, and advertisers must be able to substantiate any claims made.

Political advertising: Political advertising is subject to regulations to ensure transparency and fairness in political campaigns. These regulations may include restrictions on the use of certain types of advertising, such as ads containing false statements or ads paid for by foreign entities.

Health and safety: Advertisers must not make claims that could potentially harm the health or safety of consumers. This may include claims about the efficacy or safety of health products, or claims about the safety of vehicles or other products.

It's absolutely important for advertisers to be aware of and comply with all relevant regulations to ensure that their advertising is ethical, transparent, and effective; as discarding this or falling foul of these can lead to very expensive fines and law suits.

There are various regulations that are specific to the United Kingdom (UK) and which apply to advertising in this country. As such there are a number of bodies that have been established to regulate the U.K. advertising.

They are as follows:

The Advertising Standards Authority (ASA): The ASA is an independent regulator that is responsible for ensuring that advertising in the UK is legal, decent, honest, and truthful. The ASA has the power to take action against advertisers who breach its codes, which include rules on misleading advertising, social responsibility, and harm and offence.

CAP Code: The Committee of Advertising Practice (CAP) publishes a code that sets out the rules that advertisers must follow in the UK. The CAP Code covers areas such as misleading advertising, social responsibility, and harm and offence, and applies to all media including online and offline advertising.

Broadcast advertising: Broadcasting in the UK is regulated by the Office of Communications (Ofcom), which has rules governing the content of TV and radio advertising. These rules cover areas such as taste and decency, product placement, and political advertising.

Advertising to children: The UK has specific rules governing advertising to children, including restrictions on the use of certain types of advertising, such as ads for high-fat, salt, or sugar (HFSS) products, and requirements for clear and prominent age restrictions on ads.

Online advertising: The UK has introduced new regulations to govern online advertising, including the requirement for online platforms to ensure that ads are not placed alongside harmful or illegal content. The UK has also introduced new rules to govern the use of influencer marketing, including the requirement for influencers to clearly disclose when they have been paid to promote a product or service.

Film in Media Studies

Film is one of the main topics in the GCSE Media Studies curriculum.

It is a form of audiovisual media, that involves the recording and projection of moving images to create a narrative or tell a story. Films are typically produced for commercial or artistic purposes and are presented in cinemas, on television, or through streaming services.

Film as a form of media can be analyzed through a variety of lenses, including its narrative structure, visual style, themes, and social or political messages. Media studies scholars may examine the formal elements of films, such as their use of cinematography, sound, editing, and performance, as well as the ways in which films reflect or shape cultural attitudes and values.

Some media studies scholars also use film theory and criticism to analyze the ways in which films create meaning, engage with audiences, and reflect the societies in which they are produced. By examining film as a complex cultural and artistic medium, media studies students can gain a deeper understanding of how media shapes our experiences and perceptions of the world around us.

There are many ways to categorize films in media studies, but here are some common categories and their descriptions. Each category provides a different lens through which to analyze and understand the creative, cultural, and commercial aspects of film as a medium.

Genre: Films can be categorized by genre, which refers to the type or category of film. Some common genres include action, comedy, drama, horror, musical, science fiction, and western. Genre conventions often include certain themes, character types, plot structures, and visual styles.

Auteur: This category refers to films that are closely associated with a particular filmmaker or director, who is seen as the "author" of the film. Auteur theory emphasizes the role of the director in shaping the artistic and thematic elements of a film.

National cinema: This category refers to films produced by a particular country or region, and reflects the cultural, political, and social contexts in which they were made. National cinemas often have distinct styles, themes, and traditions that reflect their unique historical and cultural backgrounds.

Independent Films:

They are often produced by independent production companies, smaller studios, or individual filmmakers, and may be funded through private investment, grants, or other non-traditional sources.

Art house: This category refers to films that are typically made for artistic or intellectual purposes rather than commercial appeal. Art house films often have experimental or non-linear narratives, unconventional storytelling techniques, and may address philosophical or existential themes.

Period: This category refers to films that are set in a particular historical period, and often attempt to recreate the cultural, social, and political context of that time. Period films may include costume dramas, historical epics, or biopics that focus on the lives of historical figures.

Blockbuster: This category refers to films that are intended to be massive commercial successes, with high budgets, extensive marketing campaigns, and broad appeal to mainstream audiences. Blockbuster films often feature big-name stars, special effects, and action-packed plots, and are designed to generate significant box office revenue.

Documentary: This category refers to films that aim to represent reality, often through interviews, archival footage, and other forms of non-fiction storytelling. Documentaries can cover a wide range of subjects, from social issues and politics to history and science, and often offer alternative perspectives on current events or cultural phenomena.

Animated: This category refers to films that use animation techniques to create moving images, often targeting younger audiences but also appealing to adults. Animated films can include hand-drawn, computer-generated, or stop-motion animation, and often explore fantasy or science fiction themes.

Understanding Narrative in Film and Video

Narrative in film and video refers to the storytelling techniques used to convey a plot or story to the audience. It encompasses all the elements that make up a story, including characters, plot, setting, and themes.

Narrative in film and video is typically constructed through a series of shots and scenes that are edited together to create a cohesive story. The narrative can be conveyed through a variety of techniques, such as dialogue, voiceover, music, and sound effects.

The narrative structure of a film or video can take many forms, including linear, non-linear, and experimental. A linear narrative follows a chronological sequence of events, while a non-linear narrative may jump back and forth in time or use multiple perspectives to tell the story. Experimental narratives may use unconventional techniques to challenge the viewer's expectations and create a unique experience.

The narrative in film and video is an essential component of storytelling that helps to engage the audience and create a compelling experience. It can be used to explore a range of themes and ideas, and to convey complex emotions and perspectives.

Narrative codes and interventions are techniques used in film and video to construct and convey the narrative to the audience. They are tools used by filmmakers and video producers to shape the story and create meaning.

Narrative codes refer to the various techniques used to communicate meaning within a narrative, such as setting, character, dialogue, and symbolism. These codes help the audience to interpret the story and understand its underlying themes and messages.

Narrative interventions are deliberate deviations from the standard narrative codes, used to create tension, surprise, or to subvert audience expectations. For example, a sudden plot twist or unexpected character development can be an effective intervention

GCSE Media Revision Study Guide

There are several narrative codes and conventions used in film and video to construct and convey a story. Here are a few examples:

Setting: The setting of a film or video is an important narrative code that provides context and helps to establish the tone and mood of the story. This can include the physical environment, such as the location, time period, and weather.

Character: The characters in a story are another key narrative code. The protagonist is usually the central character, around whom the story revolves, and the antagonist is the character who provides conflict and obstacles for the protagonist to overcome.

Dialogue: Dialogue is a powerful narrative code that can reveal character traits, motivations, and relationships. It is used to move the story forward and create tension, conflict, and resolution.

Symbolism: Symbolism is the use of visual or auditory cues to represent abstract ideas or themes. This can include recurring motifs, metaphors, and allegories that add depth and complexity to the story.

Plot structure: The structure of the plot is another narrative convention that is used to convey the story. This includes the exposition, rising action, climax, falling action, and resolution.

Narrative techniques refer to the methods used to tell a story or convey a message in film or other media. These techniques can include:

Flashbacks: This is when a scene from the past is inserted into the present story.

Foreshadowing: This is a hint or clue about what is going to happen later in the story.

Voice-over: This is when a character's thoughts or narration is heard over the visuals.

Montage: This is when a series of shots are edited together to show the passage of time or to compress a story.

Non-linear narrative: This is when the story is told out of chronological order.

Plot twists: This is when a surprising turn of events happens that changes the direction of the story.

Symbolism: This is when objects or images are used to represent abstract ideas or concepts.

Metaphors and similes: These are literary devices used to make a comparison between two things.

Irony: This is when the opposite of what is expected happens.

Juxtaposition: This is when two contrasting images or ideas are placed side by side for effect.

These techniques are used by filmmakers to create a certain mood, build suspense, or to convey a message to the audience.

We will now look at the two major categories of films, their funding and their distribution.

Independent films

Independent films are movies that are made outside of the major Hollywood studio system, with lower budgets and greater creative control for the filmmakers. They are often produced by independent production companies, smaller studios, or individual filmmakers, and may be funded through private investment, grants, or other non-traditional sources.

Independent films often address a wide range of subjects and themes, and can include everything from small-scale dramas and comedies to experimental art films and documentaries. They may take risks with storytelling techniques or subject matter, and can provide a platform for underrepresented voices and perspectives in the film industry.

Independent filmmakers often have greater control over their creative vision and can take more risks than filmmakers working within the studio system.

They may also have a greater opportunity to experiment with new styles, techniques, and storytelling methods. However, independent films may have smaller budgets, lower production values, and may not have the same level of distribution or marketing as big-budget Hollywood movies. Nonetheless, many independent films have gained critical and commercial success, and continue to have a significant impact on the film industry.

Here are a few recent examples of independent films:

"Minari" (2020) - This drama film directed by Lee Isaac Chung follows a Korean-American family who move to Arkansas in the 1980s to start a farm. The film, which was made on a relatively low budget, received critical acclaim and was nominated for multiple Academy Awards, including Best Picture.

"Nomadland" (2020) - This drama film directed by Chloe Zhao stars Frances McDormand as a woman who, after losing everything in the Great Recession, embarks on a journey through the American West as a modern-day nomad. The film, which was produced independently, received critical acclaim and won multiple awards, including Best Picture at the 2021 Academy Awards.

"First Cow" (2019) - This drama film directed by Kelly Reichardt is set in the 1820s in the Pacific Northwest and follows two travellers who start a business selling cakes made with stolen milk from the first cow in the region. The film was praised by critics for its unique storytelling style and attention to historical detail.

"The Farewell" (2019) - This comedy-drama film directed by Lulu Wang tells the story of a Chinese-American family who decide not to tell their grandmother that she has been diagnosed with a terminal illness. The film, which was produced independently, was well-received by critics and won multiple awards.

These films, along with many others, demonstrate the creative and cultural impact that independent films can have, even with smaller budgets and distribution channels than big-budget Hollywood movies.

Funding of Independent Films

Independent films can be funded in a variety of ways, depending on the specific project and the resources available to the filmmakers. Here are a few common ways that independent films are funded:

Private investment - Independent filmmakers may seek funding from private investors, such as individuals or companies that are willing to invest money in the film in exchange for a share of the profits.

Crowdfunding - Some independent filmmakers may use crowdfunding platforms like Kickstarter or Indiegogo to raise money for their projects. This involves soliciting donations from individuals in exchange for perks or rewards, such as early access to the finished film or merchandise related to the project.

Grants - There are a variety of grants and funding programs available to independent filmmakers, particularly for projects that promote diversity, social justice, or other important issues. These grants may be offered by government agencies, foundations, or non-profit organizations.

Self-funding - Some independent filmmakers may choose to fund their projects themselves, either through personal savings or by taking on other jobs to raise money for the film.

Pre-sales - In some cases, independent filmmakers may be able to secure funding by pre-selling distribution rights to their film before it is even made. This involves negotiating contracts with distributors or streaming services who agree to distribute the film once it is completed.

Tax incentives - Some states or countries offer tax incentives to filmmakers who shoot their films in those locations. These incentives can range from rebates on expenses to tax credits that can be sold to other companies. Independent filmmakers may use these incentives as a way to lower their production costs and make their films more financially viable.

Product placement - Independent filmmakers may be able to secure funding from companies that are willing to have their products featured in the film. This can involve negotiating contracts with advertisers who agree to pay for product placement or brand integration in the film.

Co-production - Independent filmmakers may partner with other production companies, studios, or investors to share the costs and risks of making the film. Co-production agreements can involve sharing the expenses of producing the film, as well as sharing the revenues from distribution and sales.

Film festivals - Some independent filmmakers may use film festivals as a way to secure funding for their projects. This can involve submitting a short film or teaser to a festival in order to generate buzz and attract investors or distributors who are interested in the project.

International sales - Independent filmmakers may be able to generate revenue by selling distribution rights to their films in international markets. This can involve negotiating contracts with foreign distributors or streaming services who agree to distribute the film in their respective countries.

These are just a few more examples of the many ways that independent films can be funded. Ultimately, the funding strategy will depend on the specific needs and goals of the filmmakers, as well as the resources and opportunities available to them.

Independent Film Distribution

Independent films can be distributed through a variety of channels, depending on the specific project and the goals of the filmmakers. Here are a few common ways that independent films are distributed:

Theatrical release - Some independent films are released in theatres, either through a traditional distribution deal or through a self-distribution strategy. Independent filmmakers may rent out theatres themselves, or partner with independent theatres or film festivals to screen their films.

Video on demand (VOD) - Independent films may be distributed through VOD platforms, which allow viewers to rent or purchase the film online. Popular VOD platforms for independent films include Amazon Prime Video, iTunes, and Google Play.

Subscription streaming services - Independent films may also be distributed through subscription streaming services, such as Netflix or Hulu. These platforms may pay independent filmmakers a fee for the rights to stream their films, or may enter into a revenue-sharing agreement based on the number of views or subscriptions.

Film festivals - Many independent films are distributed through film festivals, which offer a platform for independent filmmakers to showcase their work to a wider audience. Festivals can also serve as a networking opportunity for filmmakers, as they may be able to connect with distributors, sales agents, or investors who are interested in the project.

Television - Some independent films may be distributed through television channels, either through a traditional broadcasting deal or through a streaming service. Independent filmmakers may negotiate contracts with cable networks or streaming services to air their films, or may partner with broadcast networks that specialize in independent or art-house films.

Studio films

Studio films are typically produced by major film studios that have significant financial resources and distribution networks. These studios often have large budgets for their films, and may invest heavily in marketing and promotion to generate buzz and interest among audiences.

Like independent films, studio films can be distributed through a variety of channels, including:

<u>Theatrical release</u> - Studio films are often released in theatres on a wide scale, with many theatres carrying the film on opening weekend. This is often accompanied by a large marketing campaign, including trailers, posters, and other promotional materials.

<u>Home video</u> - Studio films may be released on DVD or Blu-ray, allowing viewers to purchase or rent the film for home viewing. In recent years, studios have also begun to release their films on digital platforms, such as iTunes, Amazon, and Google Play.

<u>Streaming services</u> - Many studio films are also available on streaming services like Netflix, Hulu, and Amazon Prime Video. These services may pay the studio a fee for the rights to stream the film, or may enter into a revenue-sharing agreement based on the number of views or subscriptions.

<u>Television</u> - Studio films may be distributed through television channels and cable networks, either through a traditional broadcasting deal or through a streaming service.

The distribution strategy for studio films will depend on the specific goals and resources of the studio, as well as the type of film being produced. However, due to the significant resources available to studios, their films often have greater exposure and visibility than independent films.

The Marketing and Promotion of Studio film

Marketing and promotion are crucial components of the film industry, as they help to generate buzz and awareness among potential audiences. A successful marketing campaign can lead to higher box office returns, strong critical reception, and even awards recognition.

Marketing and promotion of a film typically begins long before its release date, often starting with the announcement of the project and the release of teaser trailers, posters, and other promotional materials. As the release date approaches, more extensive marketing campaigns may be launched, including trailers, social media campaigns, press tours, and other promotional events.

One of the most important marketing strategies for films is creating a strong brand identity. This can involve developing a recognizable visual style, as well as a clear and memorable tagline or slogan. For example, the tagline for the film Jaws, "You'll never go in the water again," has become an iconic part of film history.

Another key element of film marketing is creating a strong online presence. This includes promoting the film on social media platforms like Facebook, Twitter, and Instagram, as well as through online advertising and promotional content on websites and blogs.

In addition to online marketing, traditional marketing strategies like print and television advertising can also be effective for promoting films. Movie trailers are often shown on television and in theatres, and promotional posters and billboards can be displayed in high-traffic areas like bus stops and subway stations.

Finally, press coverage and reviews are important for generating buzz and building excitement for a film. Film studios may host advance screenings for critics and journalists, and may also organize press junkets and interviews with cast and crew to promote the film. Positive reviews and critical acclaim can help to build momentum for a film, while negative reviews can have the opposite effect.

A successful marketing and promotion campaign for a film requires a combination of effective branding, strong online presence, and traditional advertising and press coverage. While the specific strategies used will depend on the film, the target audience, and the resources available to the studio, a well-executed campaign can help to drive interest and excitement among potential audiences, ultimately leading to higher box office returns and critical acclaim.

Film Regulation

Film regulation involves the oversight and control of the film industry by various regulatory bodies. Film regulation can take many forms, including censorship, content classification, and the regulation of advertising and marketing materials.

It is intended to ensure that films are produced and distributed in a responsible and ethical manner. While the specific regulations and standards may vary between different countries and jurisdictions, the goal is generally to protect viewers from harmful or offensive content, while still allowing for the creative expression and freedom of speech that is central to the film industry.

Censorship

One of the most common forms of film regulation is censorship. This involves the suppression of certain content that is deemed inappropriate, offensive, or harmful to viewers. Censorship can be imposed by governments, industry bodies, or religious or moral organizations. Censorship can take various forms, including the removal of scenes or dialogue, the prohibition of certain types of content, or the outright ban of a film.

Content Classification

Another aspect of film regulation is content classification. This involves rating or categorizing films based on their content, such as violence, sex, and language. The purpose of classification is to provide guidance to viewers and parents about the appropriateness of the content for certain age groups. In the United States, the Motion Picture Association of America (MPAA) rates films using the G, PG, PG-13, R, and NC-17 ratings. Other countries have their own classification systems, which may differ in the criteria used to rate films.

Regulation of advertising and marketing materials is another important aspect of film regulation. Advertising and marketing materials for films are often subject to regulation by government agencies or industry bodies. Regulations can include guidelines on the content of trailers, posters, and other promotional materials, as well as restrictions on the placement of advertisements in certain types of media or at certain times.

The classifications are:

U – Suitable for all

PG – Parental Guidance

12A – Only used for films shown in cinemas and suitable for 12 years and over. However, people younger than 12 may see a 12A so long as they are accompanied by an adult

12 – Video release suitable for 12 years and over

15 – Suitable for only 15 years and over

18 – Suitable only for adults

MUSIC

In GCSE Media Studies, <u>music i</u>s often studied as part of the broader topic of advertising and marketing. Music is a powerful tool that can be used to influence consumer behaviour and create emotional connections between consumers and brands.

Some of the key concepts and ideas that students are expected to learn about music and marketing in GCSE Media Studies include:

<u>Brand identity</u>: Music can be used to help create and reinforce a brand's identity and some brands select specific types of music to represent their values, tone, and personality.

Emotional response: Music can elicit emotional responses in listeners, which can influence their perceptions of a brand or product. Most Advertisers use music to create specific moods or emotions that are associated with their products.

Target audience: Music can be used to appeal to specific target audiences. This is because advertisers select music that is likely to resonate with their target audience based on factors such as age, gender, and cultural background.

Licensing and copyright: Music licensing and copyright are important considerations in marketing. There are legal and ethical issues surrounding the use of music in advertising, and as such advertisers must obtain the appropriate permissions and licenses to use music in their campaigns.

Cultural context: Music is often culturally specific, and advertisers must be aware of cultural differences and sensitivities when selecting music for their campaigns in order not to cause offence.

Music Marketing

Marketing and consumption of music have undergone significant changes over the past few decades due to advancements in technology, changing consumer preferences, and the rise of social media.

The changes in music marketing and consumption over the past few years have been driven by advancements in technology and changing consumer preferences. Digital platforms and social media have enabled artists to connect with fans more easily, while also allowing fans to discover and consume music in new ways. As technology continues to evolve, it's likely that we'll see even more changes in the way music is marketed and consumed in the future.

Today, music is marketed and consumed in the following key ways and methods:

Digital Music Platforms: With the rise of digital music platforms like Spotify, Apple Music, and Amazon Music, consumers can now access millions of songs from their smartphones, tablets, and computers. These platforms use algorithms to recommend music based on users' listening habits, and allow users to create playlists and share their music with others.

Social Media: Social media platforms like Instagram, Twitter, and TikTok have become important tools for musicians to promote their music and connect with fans. Artists can use these platforms to share snippets of new songs, behind-the-scenes footage of music videos, and interact with fans in real-time.

Live Music: Live music remains an important part of the music industry, with concerts and festivals being a key revenue stream for many artists. With the growth of social media, live events have become more important than ever, as they allow artists to connect with fans in person and on social media.

Influencer Marketing: Influencer marketing has become an increasingly popular way for artists to promote their music. By partnering with social media influencers, musicians can reach new audiences and promote their music to a more diverse group of fans.

Music Videos: Music videos continue to be an important tool for marketing music, with many artists using them to tell a story or convey a message. In recent years, music videos have become more elaborate and cinematic, with some even featuring high-profile actors and directors.

Music videos are short films that are typically created to accompany a particular piece of music. They can serve a variety of purposes, including promoting a song, building an artist's image, and creating a visual narrative that complements the music.

Music videos have been around since the 1960s, but they became more popular in the 1980s with the rise of MTV. At their most basic level, music videos are a form of advertising for a particular song or artist. They aim to generate interest and excitement about the music by providing a visual component that complements the audio.

Objectives of music videos

Music videos can achieve a number of different objectives, depending on the artist and the song. Here are some common aims of music videos:

Promote the Song: One of the primary goals of a music video is to promote the song it accompanies. By creating a visual component that complements the audio, music videos can help generate interest and excitement about the song, which can lead to increased radio play, streaming, and downloads.

Build the Artist's Image: Music videos can also be used to build an artist's image and create a persona that fans can identify with. For example, a music video might portray the artist as rebellious, glamorous, or edgy, depending on the artist's brand.

Tell a Story: Some music videos are designed to tell a story that complements the song. These videos might feature a narrative that follows the lyrics of the song, or they might create a separate story that complements the mood and tone of the music.

Create a Visual Spectacle: Some music videos are designed to be visually stunning, with elaborate sets, costumes, and special effects. These videos aim to create a visual spectacle that complements the music and captures viewers' attention.

Showcase the Artist's Performance: Finally, some music videos are simply designed to showcase the artist's performance. These videos might feature footage of the artist performing the song live, or they might feature the artist lip-syncing to the recorded track in a more stylized setting.

Because Music videos are a powerful tool for promoting music and building an artist's brand, the combination of audio with visuals, can create a more immersive experience for viewers and can help establish a connection between the artist and their fans and thus makes music videos a very important aspect of the Music industry.

The different music videos

There are many different types of music videos that artists can use to promote their music and build their brand. Here are some common types of music videos:

Performance Videos: Performance videos typically feature the artist performing the song in a live setting. These videos are often shot at concerts or other live events, and can be used to showcase the artist's stage presence and performance skills.

Conceptual Videos: Conceptual videos are more abstract and experimental than narrative videos. They often use visual metaphors and other artistic techniques to convey a mood or theme that complements the music.

Animated Videos: Animated videos use animation or other forms of digital art to create a visual component for the music. These videos can be particularly effective for songs that have a strong narrative or that lend themselves to visual storytelling.

Lyric Videos: Lyric videos typically feature the lyrics of the song displayed on the screen, often in a creative and visually interesting way. These videos can be a simple and cost-effective way to promote a song, particularly if the artist doesn't have the budget for a more elaborate video.

Interactive Videos: Interactive videos allow viewers to interact with the video in some way, such as by clicking on different elements of the video or choosing different paths through the narrative. These videos can be particularly effective for engaging fans and building buzz around a new release.

Fan-Made Videos: Fan-made videos are created by fans of the artist, often using footage from concerts or other live events. While these videos are not officially sanctioned by the artist or their record label, they can be a powerful tool for building buzz and engaging fans.

Narrative Videos: Narrative videos tell a story that complements the song.

Narrative music videos can be fictional or based on real events. They can be shot in a variety of styles and genres, from cinematic dramas to stylized, abstract works of art. In many cases, narrative music videos are shot like short films, with high production values and professional actors.

The story of a narrative music video can be directly related to the lyrics of the song, or it can be more loosely connected. For example, a song about a breakup might be accompanied by a music video that tells the story of a couple going through a difficult time in their relationship. Alternatively, a song about a social issue might be accompanied by a music video that tells the story of a community coming together to address that issue.

The goal of a narrative music video is to create a visual narrative that enhances the emotional impact of the song and helps to build the artist's brand. A well-executed narrative music video can be a powerful tool for engaging fans, building buzz around a new release, and establishing the artist's visual identity.

Album cover

An album cover is the front-facing artwork or design that appears on the packaging of an album or a musical recording. Album covers can take many different forms, but they typically include the name of the artist, the album title, and some form of visual art or imagery that is intended to represent the music contained within.

Album covers can be very simple or very elaborate, depending on the artist's vision and budget. Some album covers feature a photograph of the artist or band, while others use artwork or graphic design to create a distinctive visual identity for the album.

Album covers can also play an important role in shaping the cultural impact of an album. Iconic album covers, such as the Beatles' "Sgt. Pepper's Lonely Hearts Club Band" or Pink Floyd's "The Dark Side of the Moon," have become cultural touchstones that are instantly recognizable and closely associated with the music they represent.

In recent years, the importance of album covers has evolved with the shift from physical media to digital music consumption. While album covers are still an important part of the branding and marketing of an album, they now often appear as digital images on streaming services or online music stores, rather than as physical objects that can be held and displayed.

The use of social media as a music marketing tool now

Social media has become an essential marketing tool for many businesses, including those in the music industry. Here are some ways that social media is used as a marketing tool:

Building a Fan Base: Social media platforms like Facebook, Instagram, and Twitter provide artists with a direct line of communication to their fans. By sharing behind-the-scenes content, previews of new music, and other exclusive content, artists can build a loyal fan base and keep their followers engaged.

Promoting New Releases: Social media is a powerful tool for promoting new music releases. Artists can use platforms like Instagram and TikTok to share teasers, music videos, and other promotional content in the lead-up to a new release.

Engaging Fans: Social media provides artists with a way to engage with their fans in real time. By responding to comments and messages, hosting Q&A sessions, and sharing live performances, artists can create a sense of community and deepen their connection with their fans.

Partnering with Brands: Social media can also be a way for artists to partner with brands and generate additional revenue streams. By partnering with brands that align with their brand and values, artists can create sponsored content that reaches new audiences and generates additional income.

Analyzing Data: Social media platforms also provide artists and their teams with a wealth of data about their fans and their Behaviour. By analyzing this data, artists can gain insights into their fan base and create more effective marketing strategies in the future.

Whether we approve or not, social media has become an essential marketing tool for artists and labels in the music industry. By using social media to build their fan base, promote new releases, engage with fans, partner with brands, and analyze data, artists can create a more effective and efficient marketing strategy that helps to grow their audience and build their brand.

Record Labels

Record labels are companies that specialize in the production, distribution, and marketing of music recordings. They play a crucial role in the music industry by discovering, developing, and promoting artists, as well as by investing in the production and distribution of their music.

Record labels typically sign contracts with artists, giving them the exclusive right to distribute and market their music in exchange for a percentage of the revenue generated by the recordings. In addition to providing funding for the production and promotion of new music, record labels also handle the logistics of distribution, such as pressing and shipping physical copies of albums to retailers, as well as making music available for digital download or streaming.

Record labels also typically handle the marketing and promotion of their artists. This can include everything from creating and distributing press releases and promotional materials to organizing tours, concerts, and other live events.

In recent years, the role of record labels has evolved with the rise of digital music and social media.

There are still many artists who have been able to achieve success without the support of a traditional record label, by using platforms like YouTube, SoundCloud, and TikTok to build their fan base and promote their music.

However, record labels continue to play a crucial role in the music industry, particularly for artists who are looking to reach a wider audience and achieve commercial success. While the industry has seen significant changes in recent years, record labels remain a key player in the production, distribution, and marketing of music.

The Major Record Labels in the Music Industry

There are three major record labels, also known as the "Big Three," that dominate the global music industry:

Universal Music Group: Universal Music Group (UMG) is the largest of the three major record labels, with a market share of around 30%. UMG is owned by the French media conglomerate Vivendi and has its headquarters in Santa Monica, California. UMG represents a diverse range of artists across many genres, including Taylor Swift, Billie Eilish, Drake, and Post Malone.

Sony Music Entertainment: Sony Music Entertainment is the second-largest of the major record labels, with a market share of around 22%. Sony Music is a subsidiary of the Japanese multinational conglomerate Sony Corporation and has its headquarters in New York City. Sony Music represents a wide range of artists across many genres, including Beyoncé, Travis Scott, Harry Styles, and The Chainsmokers.

Warner Music Group: Warner Music Group is the smallest of the major record labels, with a market share of around 17%. Warner Music Group is headquartered in New York City and is owned by the Access Industries conglomerate. Warner Music represents many artists across different genres, including Ed Sheeran, Cardi B, Bruno Mars, and Coldplay.

In addition to the Big Three, there are also many other record labels and independent music companies that play a significant role in the music industry, representing a diverse range of artists and genres.

EMI was once one of the major record labels and was commonly referred to as the fourth major record label, alongside Universal Music Group, Sony Music Entertainment, and Warner Music Group. However, in 2012, EMI was acquired by Universal Music Group and Sony Music Entertainment, resulting in a consolidation of the music industry and reducing the number of major record labels from four to three.

After the acquisition, EMI's assets were divided between Universal and Sony, with Universal acquiring EMI's recorded music division and Sony acquiring its publishing division. So, while EMI was once one of the major record labels, it no longer exists as an independent entity.

Independent labels

Independent labels, also known as indie labels, are record labels that operate independently from the major record labels. They are typically smaller in scale and focus on representing and promoting music that may not fit into the mainstream commercial music industry.

Independent labels may represent artists from a variety of genres, including alternative, rock, folk, hip-hop, electronic, and more. They often provide more creative freedom to their artists and offer a more personal approach to working with them.

While independent labels may not have the same level of resources as the major labels, they are often able to develop close relationships with their artists and offer a more supportive environment for their creative endeavours.

Independent labels also often have a strong focus on building a community around their music, with a dedicated fan base and a more grassroots approach to marketing and promotion.

Some well-known independent labels include Sub Pop, Domino, XL Recordings, Epitaph, Merge Records, and 4AD, among others.

The Regulation of the Music Industry

There are several music regulatory bodies that exist to regulate and oversee various aspects of the music industry. These include:

The International Federation of the Phonographic Industry (IFPI): The IFPI is the global trade association for the recording industry. It represents the interests of record labels and music companies around the world, and works to promote the value of recorded music, protect the rights of creators and copyright owners, and support the growth and development of the music industry.

The Recording Industry Association of America (RIAA): The RIAA is a trade organization that represents the major record labels in the United States. It works to protect the intellectual property rights of its members, promote the value of music, and combat piracy and copyright infringement.

The Performing Rights Society (PRS): The PRS is a UK-based organization that represents the interests of songwriters, composers, and music publishers. It collects and distributes royalties on behalf of its members for the use of their music in various contexts, such as radio and television broadcasts, live performances, and digital platforms.

The American Society of Composers, Authors and Publishers (ASCAP): ASCAP is a US-based organization that represents the interests of songwriters, composers, and music publishers. It works to protect the rights of its members, collect and distribute royalties for the use of their music, and provide a range of services and resources to support their creative careers.

The Copyright Office: The Copyright Office is a US government agency that is responsible for administering copyright law in the United States. It registers and catalogs copyrightable works, provides information and guidance on copyright law and policy, and works to promote the protection of creative works and the rights of copyright owners.

Newspapers

Newspapers are an important aspect of the GCSE Media curriculum, as they provide a key example of print media and how it has evolved over time.

In GCSE Media, you will study newspapers in terms of their ownership, production, and distribution, as well as their content and how it reflects social, cultural, and political issues. You may also analyze the role of newspapers in shaping public opinion, and how they have adapted to changes in technology and the rise of digital media.

When studying newspapers, you will be asked to analyze various elements of their content, such as headlines, bylines, photographs, captions, and articles, as well as the layout and design of the newspaper as a whole. You may also be asked to consider the different genres of news, such as hard news, feature stories, opinion pieces, and editorials, and how these reflect different aspects of society and culture.

It is important to note the role of advertising in newspapers, and how it is used to generate revenue and shape consumer Behaviour. You should analyze the techniques and strategies used in advertising, and how they reflect the values and priorities of society as this will provide you with a deeper understanding of how print media operates, and how it has evolved and adapted over time. It will also help you to develop critical thinking skills and the ability to analyze and evaluate media content in a thoughtful and nuanced way.

Types of Newspapers

There are several types of newspapers, which can be broadly classified based on their content, audience, and format. Some of the most common types of newspapers include:

<u>Broadsheet newspapers</u>: These are larger format newspapers that traditionally featured serious news and editorial content. They are typically read by a more educated and affluent audience.

Tabloid newspapers: These are smaller format newspapers that are often more sensational in their content and appeal to a broader, more populist audience. They may also have a greater focus on celebrity news and gossip.

Regional newspapers: These are newspapers that cover news and events in a particular geographic region or area, such as a city or county.

National newspapers: These are newspapers that cover news and events on a national level, and are typically distributed across the entire country.

Specialty newspapers: These are newspapers that cater to a specific niche or interest group, such as sports fans, business professionals, or hobbyists.

Online newspapers: These are newspapers that are published exclusively online, and may include both original content and articles from other sources.

Free newspapers: These are newspapers that are distributed for free, often through public transportation or in public places like cafes and libraries. They are typically funded by advertising revenue.

Each type of newspaper has a different focus and tone, and is designed to appeal to a specific audience or demographic.

Newspaper Language

Newspaper language, also known as journalism or news writing, it is a distinct style of writing that is tailored to the unique needs and constraints of the newspaper industry. It is designed to be informative, concise, and engaging, while also maintaining a sense of accuracy and objectivity.

Some of the key features of newspaper language include:

Inverted pyramid structure: This refers to the practice of placing the most important information at the beginning of an article, and then gradually working down to less important details.

Headlines: These are short, attention-grabbing titles that are designed to summarize the key points of an article and entice readers to read on.

Short paragraphs: Newspaper articles are typically broken up into short paragraphs, often just one or two sentences long. This helps to make the content more readable and easier to scan.

Direct quotes: Newspaper articles often include direct quotes from sources, which help to add depth and credibility to the content.

Objectivity: Newspaper articles are typically written in a neutral, objective tone, without expressing personal opinions or bias.

Clarity: Newspaper language is designed to be clear and easy to understand, with simple sentence structures and straightforward vocabulary.

Photographs in Media Studies

Photographs are an important part of newspaper language, as they can help to add context and visual interest to news stories. In a newspaper context, photographs are typically used to illustrate news stories, and may include images of people, places, or events.

Some of the key considerations when using photographs in a newspaper context include:

Relevance: The photograph should be relevant to the story and help to add context or information that is not conveyed through text.

Quality: The photograph should be clear and well-composed, with good lighting and focus.

Copyright: Newspapers must be careful to ensure that they have the legal right to use any photographs they publish, and should obtain permission or pay a licensing fee when necessary.

Ethical considerations: Newspapers should be mindful of any potential ethical considerations when using photographs, such as respecting the privacy of individuals or avoiding images that may be offensive or triggering.

In addition to photographs, newspapers may also use other types of visual elements to enhance their stories, such as infographics, charts, and illustrations. These visual elements can help to convey complex information in a clear and accessible way, and may be particularly useful for topics like science or economics.

Headlines in Media Studies

Headlines are short, attention-grabbing titles that appear at the top of news articles in newspapers, magazines, and online news sources. They are designed to quickly and succinctly summarize the key points of the article and entice readers to read on.

Headlines are an important part of newspaper language, as they help to attract readers and draw attention to important news stories. A well-written headline can make the difference between a reader choosing to read an article or moving on to something else.

Effective headlines are usually short, typically no more than 10-12 words, and use active language and strong verbs to create a sense of urgency or excitement. They may also use puns, wordplay, or other forms of clever language to capture readers' attention.

Some common features of headlines include:

Clarity: Headlines should be clear and easy to understand, even for readers who are unfamiliar with the topic or subject matter.

Accuracy: Headlines should accurately reflect the content of the article and avoid any exaggeration or hyperbole.

Tone: Headlines should match the tone of the article, whether that is serious and informative or light-hearted and humourous.

Keyword optimization: In online news sources, headlines may be optimized for search engines by including keywords that users are likely to search for.

Timing: In breaking news situations, headlines may be updated frequently to reflect new information as it becomes available.

.

Tabloid headlines

Tabloid headlines are a type of newspaper headline that is typically associated with tabloid-style newspapers, which are known for their sensationalist and often exaggerated coverage of news stories. Tabloid headlines are designed to be attention-grabbing and provocative, and often use language that is emotive, confrontational, or scandalous.

They are a controversial aspect of newspaper language, as some people see them as entertaining and attention-grabbing, while others see them as sensationalist and untrustworthy. It's important for readers to approach tabloid headlines with a critical eye and be aware of the potential for bias or exaggeration

Some common features of tabloid headlines include:

Sensationalism: Tabloid headlines are often designed to exaggerate or sensationalize news stories in order to make them seem more exciting or scandalous.

Emotion: Tabloid headlines may use emotional language or appeal to readers' fears, anxieties, or prejudices in order to create a strong emotional response.

Wordplay: Tabloid headlines may use puns, alliteration, or other forms of wordplay to make them more memorable or catchy.

Celebrities: Tabloid headlines often focus on celebrities or other public figures, and may use their names or images to attract readers' attention.

Bias: Tabloid headlines may be biased or one-sided, and may present news stories in a way that reflects the newspaper's political or social agenda.

Broadsheet Headlines

Broadsheet headlines are a type of newspaper headline that is typically associated with broadsheet-style newspapers, which are known for their more serious and in-depth coverage of news stories. Broadsheet headlines are designed to convey the key points of the article in a concise and informative way, while also reflecting the newspaper's editorial values and priorities.

They are an important part of newspaper language, as they help to convey the key points of news stories in a clear and informative way. They are typically more serious and objective than tabloid headlines, reflecting the editorial values and priorities of broadsheet-style newspapers.

Some common features of broadsheet headlines include:

Clarity: Broadsheet headlines are typically written in a clear and concise style that emphasizes the main point or angle of the article.

Objectivity: Broadsheet headlines are often written in an objective, impartial style that avoids emotive language or bias.

Informative: Broadsheet headlines aim to provide readers with information, often focusing on news stories that are of national or international importance.

Analysis: Broadsheet headlines may also include a level of analysis or interpretation, helping readers to understand the significance of the news story in a broader context.

Length: Broadsheet headlines are often longer than tabloid headlines, as they aim to convey more information and context.

The News

News can come from a variety of sources, including:

News agencies: News agencies such as Reuters, Associated Press, and Agence France-Presse gather news stories from around the world and distribute them to newspapers, broadcasters, and online news sites.

Journalists: Professional journalists working for newspapers, TV stations, and online news outlets gather news through a variety of methods, including interviews, research, and on-the-ground reporting.

Press releases: Organizations and individuals can issue press releases to announce news and events to the media.

Social media: Increasingly, news is being shared and reported on social media platforms such as Twitter, Facebook, and Instagram.

Eyewitnesses: People who witness news events firsthand can share their experiences and footage with the media.

Government agencies: Government agencies such as the police, military, and intelligence services can provide information and updates on news stories.

It is important for journalists and news consumers alike to critically evaluate the reliability and accuracy of the sources they rely on.

News Value:

News value refers to the criteria that journalists and news editors use to determine whether a story is newsworthy and should be covered by the media. News value is a set of factors that make a story interesting and relevant to the audience.

It is a set of criteria that helps journalists and news editors decide which stories to cover and how to present them to the audience.

Some common news values include:

Timeliness: Stories that are happening right now or have just happened are considered more newsworthy than stories that are not time-sensitive.

Proximity: Stories that are happening close to the audience are considered more relevant and interesting than stories that are happening far away.

Significance: Stories that have a significant impact on people's lives, such as major political or economic events, are considered more newsworthy than less important stories.

Conflict: Stories that involve conflict, controversy, or drama are often considered more interesting and engaging than stories that do not.

Novelty: Stories that are unusual or unexpected, such as scientific breakthroughs or celebrity scandals, are often considered more newsworthy than routine stories.

Human interest: Stories that involve human emotion, such as personal triumphs or tragedies, are often considered more compelling and memorable than stories that do not.

Marketing and Distributing Newspapers

Newspapers are marketed and distributed in a variety of ways, depending on the publication and the market it serves. Here are some common methods:

Subscription: Many newspapers offer subscriptions, where readers can sign up to receive the newspaper on a daily, weekly, or monthly basis. Subscribers usually receive the newspaper in the mail or through a newspaper delivery service.

Newsstands: Newspapers are often sold at newsstands and convenience stores, where readers can purchase a copy on the spot. Newsstands are usually located in busy urban areas, such as train stations and airports.

Online: Many newspapers now have websites where readers can access articles and other content online. Some newspapers offer digital subscriptions, where readers can access the full content of the newspaper online for a fee.

Free distribution: Some newspapers are distributed for free, either through direct mail or through distribution points such as coffee shops or libraries. These newspapers often rely on advertising revenue to support their operations.

Partnership distribution: Some newspapers partner with other businesses or organizations to distribute their publications. For example, a local newspaper might be distributed at a tourist information center or at a sports stadium.

In terms of marketing, newspapers often use a mix of advertising and promotion to attract readers and advertisers. This might include print and online advertising, social media promotion, and special events or promotions.

Online newspapers

Online newspapers, also known as digital newspapers or e-papers, are newspapers that are published online and can be accessed through the internet. Online newspapers have become increasingly popular in recent years, as more and more people turn to the internet for news and information.

There are several advantages to online newspapers. For one, they are often free to access, which makes them more accessible to a wider audience. Online newspapers also allow for more up-to-date news coverage, as they can be updated in real-time as events unfold. They also often provide more multimedia content, such as videos, audio clips, and interactive graphics, which can enhance the reader's experience.

In terms of marketing and distribution, online newspapers often use search engine optimization (SEO) techniques to increase their visibility and attract readers. They also use social media platforms to promote their content and engage with readers. Some online newspapers have paywalls, where readers are required to pay a subscription fee to access premium content.

However, online newspapers also face some challenges. For one, they rely heavily on advertising revenue, which can be unpredictable and subject to fluctuations in the market. They also face competition from other online news sources, such as blogs and social media, which can make it difficult to stand out and attract readers. Additionally, there are concerns about the impact of online news on traditional print newspapers, which have seen declining circulation and revenue in recent years.

Newspapers Ownership

Newspapers can be owned by individuals, companies, or groups. Ownership can have a significant impact on the content and editorial direction of the newspaper, as well as its financial stability and business practices.

The following are some common types of newspaper ownership:

<u>Individual ownership</u>: Some newspapers are owned by individual entrepreneurs or families. These owners can have a strong influence on the editorial direction and content of the newspaper, and may be motivated by personal or ideological interests.

<u>Corporate ownership</u>: Many newspapers are owned by large corporations or media conglomerates. Corporate ownership can provide financial stability and resources, but can also lead to a focus on profits and a potential conflict of interest with the newspaper's editorial independence.

Non-profit ownership: Some newspapers are owned by non-profit organizations or foundations. These owners are often focused on promoting a particular cause or supporting public interest journalism, and may not be driven by profits.

Government ownership: In some countries, newspapers are owned by the government or state. This can raise concerns about censorship and government influence on the media.

The ownership of a newspaper can also impact its distribution and marketing strategies. For example, a newspaper owned by a large corporation might have access to a wider distribution network and greater marketing resources than a small, independently-owned newspaper.

It's important to note that ownership of newspapers is not always straightforward, and can involve complex corporate structures and relationships. Additionally, the issue of ownership is often intertwined with larger debates about media ownership and concentration of power in the media industry.

Radio

Radio is a form of broadcasting that uses radio waves to transmit information, including music, news, and talk shows. Radio has been a popular medium of communication and entertainment for over a century, and continues to be used extensively today.

Radio is typically broadcast through radio stations, which can be either commercial or non-commercial. Commercial radio stations are often owned by media companies and generate revenue through advertising, while non-commercial radio stations are often run by non-profit organizations or educational institutions.

Radio is used for a wide range of purposes, including entertainment, news, education, and emergency communication. Many people listen to the radio in their cars, at home, or at work, and it remains a popular source of music and other audio content.

In recent years, radio has adapted to changes in technology and consumer Behaviour. The rise of digital radio has allowed listeners to access radio content online, through mobile apps, and through smart speakers. Additionally, the use of podcasts and other on-demand audio content has become increasingly popular, allowing listeners to choose what they want to listen to and when.

Radio is also used extensively in advertising and marketing. Radio ads are often targeted to specific demographics and geographic areas, and can be an effective way for businesses to reach potential customers.

Overall, radio remains a popular and important medium of communication and entertainment, and continues to adapt to changes in technology and consumer Behaviour.

Pirate Radio Stations

Pirate radio stations are unlicensed radio stations that operate outside the legal framework of the broadcasting industry. These stations broadcast on radio frequencies without obtaining a license from the relevant government regulatory agency, and often operate from mobile or makeshift studios.

Pirate radio stations have been around since the early days of radio broadcasting, and have often been associated with countercultural movements or underground music scenes. In some cases, pirate radio stations have played an important role in promoting new or marginalized forms of music and culture that might not otherwise have been heard on mainstream radio.

However, pirate radio stations can also be controversial, as they can interfere with licensed radio stations and potentially pose a risk to public safety. For this reason, many countries have strict laws and regulations governing radio broadcasting, and illegal pirate radio stations can face legal action or even criminal charges.

In recent years, the rise of internet radio and online streaming has provided new opportunities for independent and alternative radio broadcasting, without the need for expensive licenses or broadcasting equipment. While pirate radio stations still exist in some parts of the world, the growth of online broadcasting has made it easier for individuals and communities to create their own radio content and reach a global audience without breaking the law.

One example of a prominent pirate radio station is Radio Caroline, which was established in the UK in the 1960s. Radio Caroline was one of the first pirate radio stations in the UK, and played an important role in promoting new forms of music, including rock and roll and pop.

At the time, the UK government had strict laws that effectively banned commercial radio broadcasting, in order to protect the monopoly of the BBC. However, many young people were interested in hearing new and diverse forms of music that were not being played on the BBC.

Radio Caroline operated from a ship that was anchored in international waters off the coast of the UK, in order to avoid British law. The station was run by a group of passionate music enthusiasts who were dedicated to promoting new forms of music and culture.

Despite facing regular harassment and attempts to shut it down by the UK government, Radio Caroline remained popular and influential throughout the 1960s and 1970s. The station played a key role in promoting the British rock music scene, and helped to establish many new bands and artists.

While Radio Caroline eventually obtained a license to broadcast legally in the UK in the 1990s, it remains an important symbol of the role that pirate radio stations can play in promoting independent music and culture.

Other Technological Innovations

There have also been many technological innovations in the field of radio broadcasting. One of the most significant recent innovations is the development of digital radio, which uses digital signals rather than traditional analog signals to transmit radio broadcasts.

Digital radio offers many advantages over analog radio, including higher sound quality, more reliable signal transmission, and the ability to transmit additional data alongside the audio signal. Digital radio also allows for more efficient use of radio spectrum, which can reduce the cost and complexity of broadcasting.

Another recent innovation in radio broadcasting is the use of internet radio and online streaming. Internet radio allows broadcasters to reach a global audience without the need for expensive broadcast licenses or infrastructure. This has led to a proliferation of independent and alternative radio stations, which can provide diverse and niche programming that might not be available on traditional broadcast radio.

Advances in mobile technology have also had a significant impact on radio broadcasting. Many smartphones and mobile devices now include built-in FM radio receivers, which allow users to listen to traditional FM radio broadcasts on the go. In addition, many streaming services and apps now offer personalized radio stations and on-demand audio content, which can be accessed from anywhere with an internet connection.

These technological innovations have expanded the reach and diversity of radio broadcasting, and have opened up new opportunities for independent and alternative radio programming.

Radio Brand

Radio brand refers to the unique identity and image that a radio station creates and promotes in order to distinguish itself from other radio stations and attract listeners. A radio brand encompasses many different elements, including the station's name, logo, tagline, programming, personalities, and overall tone and style.

Creating a strong and recognizable brand is important for radio stations because it can help them stand out in a crowded and competitive marketplace. A strong brand can also help to build a loyal audience and establish a sense of community around the station.

To create a successful radio brand, stations often invest in marketing and promotion, including advertising campaigns, social media outreach, and events and sponsorships. They may also conduct market research to better understand their target audience and tailor their programming and marketing efforts accordingly.

Ultimately, a radio brand is about creating a unique and compelling identity that resonates with listeners and helps to establish a strong and lasting connection with them.

Marketing in Radio

Radio stations use a variety of marketing strategies to promote their brand and attract listeners. Here are some common methods used by radio stations to market themselves:

Advertising: Radio stations often advertise on other media platforms, such as TV, print, or online, to reach a wider audience and raise awareness of their brand.

On-air promotion: Radio stations use on-air promotions to encourage listeners to tune in and engage with the station. This might include contests, giveaways, or special programming events.

Social media: Radio stations use social media platforms, such as Facebook, Twitter, and Instagram, to engage with listeners, promote their brand, and share content.

Email marketing: Radio stations use email newsletters to communicate with their listeners, promote upcoming events or programming, and offer exclusive content or promotions.

Partnerships and sponsorships: Radio stations may partner with local businesses, events, or organizations to promote their brand and reach new audiences.

Street team marketing: Radio stations often have a team of ambassadors who promote the station at events, concerts, or on the street. They might distribute promotional materials, host games or contests, or offer free merchandise.

Radio stations use a mix of traditional and digital marketing strategies to reach their target audience and promote their brand. By engaging with listeners, offering compelling content, and creating a unique identity, radio stations can build a loyal and dedicated audience.

Media Websites

Websites are incredibly important for media companies because they provide a central hub for all of their content and allow them to reach a global audience. Here are some of the key reasons why websites are so important for media companies:

Reach: Websites allow media companies to reach a wider audience than traditional print or broadcast media. With a website, media companies can publish content that can be accessed from anywhere in the world, 24/7.

Engagement: Websites allow media companies to engage with their audience in new and innovative ways. They can use interactive features such as comments, forums, and social media integration to encourage their audience to participate in the conversation and share their opinions.

Branding: Websites provide a platform for media companies to establish and promote their brand. They can use their website to showcase their unique voice, visual identity, and values, and to build a loyal audience that identifies with their brand.

Analytics: Websites provide media companies with valuable data on their audience, such as demographics, location, and Behaviour. This data can be used to inform content strategy, advertising decisions, and other business decisions.

Revenue: Websites can provide media companies with new revenue streams, such as advertising, subscriptions, and e-commerce. They can also help to reduce costs associated with traditional print or broadcast media, such as printing and distribution.

Standard Practices

The codes and conventions of websites refer to the standard practices and design elements that are commonly used to create effective and user-friendly websites. Here are some of the most important codes and conventions of websites:

Navigation: Effective website navigation is essential for helping users find the content they're looking for quickly and easily. Common navigation elements include menus, drop-downs, and breadcrumbs.

Layout: The layout of a website should be clean, clear, and easy to follow. This typically involves using a grid-based layout, with clear sections and headings to help users navigate the content.

Typography: Typography refers to the use of fonts and text formatting to enhance the readability and visual appeal of a website. Common practices include using a legible font, using headings and subheadings to break up the content, and using font sizes and weights to create hierarchy.

Imagery: Images and graphics can be used to enhance the visual appeal of a website and make it more engaging for users. Common practices include using high-quality images, using relevant and engaging graphics, and optimizing images for fast loading times.

Branding: Websites should reflect the branding and visual identity of the media company or organization. This typically involves using the company's logo and colour scheme consistently throughout the website.

Accessibility: Websites should be designed with accessibility in mind, ensuring that they are usable and easy to navigate for users with disabilities. Common practices include using clear and concise language, providing alt text for images, and ensuring that the website is compatible with assistive technologies.

Content convergence

Content convergence refers to the phenomenon of different types of media content, such as text, images, audio, and video, being made available through a single platform or device. It involves the integration of various media formats and technologies to create a seamless and immersive user experience.

For example, content convergence can be seen in the way that traditional media companies have expanded their offerings to include digital media, such as websites and mobile apps, that allow users to access a variety of content types in one place. It can also be seen in the way that social media platforms have evolved to include multimedia content, such as videos and live streams, alongside traditional text-based content.

It is driven by advances in technology and changing consumer preferences for more immersive and interactive media experiences. It also has significant implications for the media industry, as it requires media companies to adapt to new platforms and technologies in order to remain competitive and reach their audiences effectively.

Video Games

Video games and computers play an increasingly important role in media, as they provide a platform for interactive entertainment and communication.

Video games are a form of interactive media that allow users to engage with virtual worlds and characters. They can be played on a variety of devices, including consoles, computers, and mobile devices, and can take many different forms, including action, adventure, puzzle, and role-playing games.

Computers, on the other hand, are a ubiquitous tool used for a variety of media-related tasks, including digital media production, communication, and consumption. They are essential for tasks such as editing video and audio, designing graphics and animations, and creating websites and other digital content.

The use of video games and computers in media has opened up new opportunities for interactive storytelling, immersive experiences, and social engagement. For example, some video games allow players to make choices that affect the outcome of the story, while others allow players to interact with other players in real-time through online multiplayer modes.

Computers and video games have also transformed the way that media is distributed and consumed, as digital media files can be easily downloaded and shared over the internet. This has enabled new business models, such as digital distribution and online streaming, which have disrupted traditional media industries and created new opportunities for content creators and consumers alike.

Video games and computers are important components of the modern media landscape, offering unique opportunities for interactive entertainment, communication, and creative expression.

There are many video game producers currently in the industry, ranging from large multinational corporations to small independent studios. Some of the biggest and most well-known video game producers include:

Electronic Arts (EA)

Activision Blizzard

Ubisoft

Take-Two Interactive

Nintendo

Sony Interactive Entertainment

Microsoft Game Studios

Tencent Games

Square Enix

Bethesda Softworks

These companies produce a wide range of video games, from blockbuster franchises like Call of Duty and FIFA to innovative indie titles like Celeste and Hollow Knight. In addition to these major producers, there are also thousands of smaller studios around the world creating their own unique games and pushing the boundaries of the medium.

Video games are used in a variety of ways, from entertainment to education and even therapy. Here are some examples:

Entertainment: The primary use of video games is for entertainment purposes. People play games to have fun, relax, and escape from reality for a while.

Education: Video games are increasingly being used as educational tools. Games can be designed to teach a variety of skills, such as problem-solving, critical thinking, and language learning.

Training: Video games are also used for training purposes, particularly in fields such as the military, aviation, and healthcare. Simulations can help train people for high-stress situations without putting them in danger.

Therapy: Video games are being used to treat a variety of mental health conditions, including depression, anxiety, and PTSD. Games can be designed to help people cope with difficult emotions and develop new coping skills.

Socialization: Video games can also be used as a way to socialize with others. Multiplayer games allow people to connect with others who share similar interests and form new friendships.

Video games are marketed in a variety of ways, including:

Trailers and previews: Game developers often release trailers and previews of their upcoming games to generate hype and build anticipation.

Social media: Social media platforms like Twitter, Facebook, and Instagram are often used to promote upcoming games, share news and updates, and engage with fans.

Reviews and press coverage: Gaming websites and publications often review new games and provide coverage of gaming events like E3 and Gamescom. Positive reviews and coverage can help generate buzz and increase sales.

Influencer marketing: Game developers often partner with popular YouTubers, Twitch streamers, and other online influencers to promote their games to their audiences.

Events and conventions: Gaming events like PAX, E3, and Gamescom are important marketing opportunities for game developers. These events allow developers to showcase their games to a large audience and generate buzz among fans and press.

Demos and betas: Developers may release demos or betas of their games to allow players to try them out before they are released. This can generate interest and excitement among players, and can also provide valuable feedback for developers to improve their games before release.

Just as in Albums; cover art is an important part of marketing video games. It serves as the first visual representation of the game that potential customers see, and can influence their decision to purchase the game.

The cover art of a video game usually features key elements of the game, such as the main character, important objects or locations, or iconic moments from the game. The artwork is designed to be eye-catching and memorable, and may incorporate bold colours, dynamic action, and striking imagery to capture the attention of potential buyers.

In addition to the artwork itself, the design of the cover may also include important information such as the game's title, developer and publisher logos, rating and age restrictions, and any notable awards or accolades the game has received.

Cover art is also important for establishing the identity of a game franchise. Consistent cover art design across multiple games can create a recognizable brand image that helps customers identify and connect with the franchise.

In some cases, different regions may have different cover art for the same game. This may be due to cultural differences or marketing strategies aimed at different target audiences. For example, a game marketed primarily towards young children may have a different cover in a region where different themes or characters are popular.

Regulations in the UK

In the UK, video games are regulated by the Video Standards Council Rating Board (VSCRB), which is responsible for classifying video games according to their content and age appropriateness. The VSCRB provides age ratings for video games in the UK based on a number of factors, including violence, sexual content, language, and drug use.

The ratings provided by the VSCRB are as follows:

PEGI 3: Suitable for all ages

PEGI 7: Recommended for children aged 7 and older

PEGI 12: Suitable for children aged 12 and older

PEGI 16: Suitable for players aged 16 and older

PEGI 18: Recommended for adults aged 18 and older

These ratings are legally enforced in the UK, and retailers are prohibited from selling video games to customers who are underage for the rating of the game.

The VSCRB also provides content descriptors for each game, which give more specific information about the content of the game. These descriptors include violence, language, sex, drugs, discrimination, fear, and gambling.

In addition to the VSCRB ratings, the UK government has also introduced regulations aimed at reducing the harmful effects of video games on children, such as limiting the amount of time children can spend playing games and requiring parental controls on gaming devices.

Genres and subgenres are categories used to classify video games, the same as for film. They are based on a common characteristics and themes.

A genre refers to a broad category of media that share common elements such as plot, setting, characters, and style. For example, in film, some common genres are action, comedy, drama, horror, romance, science fiction, and westerns.

Subgenres, on the other hand, are more specific categories within a broader genre. They are usually distinguished by unique features or themes that are not common to all works within the broader genre. For example, within the horror genre, there are subgenres such as slasher, supernatural, psychological, and zombie.

Some genres and subgenres in different forms of media are:

Film: Action, adventure, animation, comedy, crime, drama, fantasy, horror, musical, romance, science fiction, thriller, western.

Television: Sitcom, drama, documentary, reality TV, news, game shows, soap operas, crime, science fiction, comedy, horror.

Music: Pop, rock, hip hop, R&B, jazz, country, classical, electronic, alternative, heavy metal.

Literature: Fiction, non-fiction, poetry, drama, mystery, romance, science fiction, fantasy, horror, biography.

Video games: Action, adventure, role-playing, sports, simulation, strategy, puzzle, survival, horror.

Hybrid genres

Hybrid genres are categories that combine elements from multiple genres and subgenres to create a unique style or theme. Hybrid genres can be found in various forms of media such as film, television, literature, music, and video games.

Some examples of hybrid genres are:

Romantic comedy: A film genre that combines elements of romantic and comedy genres.

Action-adventure: A video game genre that combines elements of action and adventure genres.

Science fiction horror: A film genre that combines elements of science fiction and horror genres.

Historical fiction: A literary genre that combines fictional elements with historical events and characters.

Reality competition: A television genre that combines reality and game show elements.

Hybrid genres can provide a fresh and unique experience for audiences and can also appeal to a wider range of viewers or players who enjoy multiple genres.

Representation

In GCSE media studies, representation refers to the way that social groups, individuals, events, and ideas are presented in media texts such as films, television programmes, newspapers, and advertisements. Representation is not a simple reflection of reality, but rather it is a constructed image that is influenced by cultural and social factors, such as power, stereotypes, and dominant ideologies.

Representation can be examined through a range of media language tools, including camera angles, lighting, sound, editing, and mise-en-scène. These tools can be used to create particular meanings and interpretations of the people, events, and ideas represented in the media text. It is important to analyse the representation of different social groups and individuals in the media, and to question the ways in which particular groups are stereotyped, underrepresented, or misrepresented.

Representation in media is constructed through a variety of methods, which include but are not limited to:

Stereotyping: Stereotypes are oversimplified and widely held beliefs about a group or individual that do not take into account the diversity within that group or individual.

Language: The choice of language used to describe a person or group can reinforce or challenge stereotypes.

Mise-en-scène: This refers to the visual aspects of a scene, such as the setting, props, and lighting, which can convey specific messages and meanings.

Camera angles and shots: The way a camera is positioned and the type of shot used can have an impact on the representation of a character or group.

Editing: The way a film or television programme is edited can shape the representation of the characters and the narrative.

Sound and music: Sound can be used to create a certain mood or atmosphere, while music can also influence how a character or group is represented.

Narrative structure: The way a story is structured can have an impact on the representation of characters and groups.

It is important to note that representation is not objective, and is influenced by the cultural and social contexts in which media texts are produced and consumed. Therefore, it is important to critically analyse and question the representation of different social groups and individuals in the media.

Representation of gender refers to the ways in which gender roles, identities, and characteristics are portrayed in media. This includes the representation of both male and female characters in various forms of media, such as television shows, films, advertisements, and news reports.

Media can represent gender in a number of ways, ranging from reinforcing traditional gender stereotypes to challenging them. For example, traditional representations of gender often portray men as strong, aggressive, and dominant, while women are typically shown as nurturing, emotional, and submissive. However, more recent representations of gender have attempted to subvert these traditional gender roles and challenge these stereotypes by portraying more diverse and nuanced representations of men and women.

It's important to note that representations of gender in media can have a significant impact on individuals' beliefs, attitudes, and Behaviours regarding gender. For this reason, media literacy and critical analysis of media representations of gender are essential skills for students in media studies.

A Case Study of the Representation of Gender in the Media

In the #MeToo movement, which started in 2017 as a social media campaign to bring awareness to sexual harassment and assault. The movement gained momentum and spread globally, leading to a number of high-profile cases being brought to light and resulting in a shift in the way that gender is represented in media.

The movement highlighted the prevalence of sexual harassment and assault in industries such as film and television, where women have traditionally been underrepresented both on and off screen. The movement also brought attention to the gender pay gap and the lack of opportunities for women in leadership positions in these industries.

As a result of the movement, there have been significant changes in the way that gender is represented in media, with more attention being given to the stories and perspectives of women and other marginalized groups. There has also been a shift towards more diverse and inclusive casting and hiring practices, as well as greater accountability for those who engage in sexual harassment and assault.

The #MeToo movement is a powerful example of how representation in media can have a real-world impact and bring about positive change.

The representation of age in media refers to how individuals of different ages are portrayed and depicted in media texts such as films, TV shows, advertisements, and magazines.

In media, young people are often portrayed as energetic, attractive, and carefree, while older people are often portrayed as wise, experienced, and in need of support. These representations can have a significant impact on how people perceive themselves and others.

There are many examples of representation of age in media, such as the portrayal of older adults in the film "The Best Exotic Marigold Hotel" as being adventurous and seeking new experiences, or the portrayal of young people in advertisements for clothing as being trendy and fashionable. However, there can also be negative representations, such as the stereotypical portrayal of older people as being frail and dependent, or the stereotypical portrayal of teenagers as being rebellious and disrespectful.

It is important for media to accurately represent people of all ages and avoid harmful stereotypes.

An example of age representation in media is the way older adults are portrayed in advertising. Historically, older adults have been depicted as frail and dependent, but in recent years, there has been a shift towards more positive representations. One notable example is the "Get a Mac" ad campaign from Apple in the 2000s, which featured John Hodgman as a bumbling PC and Justin Long as a cool, young Mac. The campaign positioned Mac as the hip, modern choice and PC as the outdated, uncool option. In response, Microsoft launched its own ad campaign featuring an older couple named "Bill" and "Shirley," who were depicted as hip and tech-savvy despite their age. This campaign challenged the negative stereotypes of older adults and portrayed them as capable and modern.

In media studies, ethnic, national, and regional identity refers to the representation of groups of people based on their ethnicity, nationality, or geographic region in various forms of media. This representation can be positive, negative, or stereotypical and can influence how these groups are perceived by the wider society.

Ethnic identity in media refers to the portrayal of people from specific ethnic groups, such as Black, Hispanic, Asian, or Indigenous peoples. This representation can either challenge or reinforce stereotypes and prejudices, and can have a significant impact on how these groups are perceived by the public. An example is A TV show that focuses on the experiences of a particular ethnic group, such as "Fresh Off the Boat," which centers on a Taiwanese-American family.

National identity refers to the representation of people based on their country of origin, and can be expressed through various symbols, such as flags, anthems, and landmarks. The representation of national identity in media can help foster a sense of patriotism and pride in one's country, but it can also reinforce nationalistic attitudes and promote prejudices against other countries and cultures. An example is A movie that celebrates the history or culture of a particular country, such as "Braveheart," which is about Scottish hero William Wallace.

Regional identity refers to the representation of people from specific geographic regions, such as cities, states, or provinces. This representation can include specific accents, dialects, customs, and traditions that are associated with that region. The representation of regional identity in media can help to celebrate and preserve local cultures, but it can also reinforce stereotypes and prejudices against people from other regions. An example is A TV show or movie that represents a particular region of a country, such as "Breaking Bad," which is set and filmed in New Mexico and features many local landmarks and cultural references.

The representation of ethnic, national, and regional identity in media can have a significant impact on how people view themselves and others, and it is important for media producers to be aware of the potential effects of their portrayals.

Target audience refers to the specific group of people for whom a particular media product, such as a film, television show, or advertisement, is intended. The target audience can be defined by a number of factors, including demographics such as age, gender, race, socioeconomic status, and geographic location, as well as psychographics such as attitudes, values, and interests.

In media studies, understanding the target audience is important for producers and marketers because it can help them to create content that resonates with the intended audience and is therefore more likely to be successful. For example, a children's television show will have a very different target audience than a crime drama, and producers will use different narrative and visual techniques to appeal to each audience.

Identifying the target audience can also be useful for advertisers, who can use demographic and psychographic data to create more effective ad campaigns. For example, a car company targeting young, urban professionals might create ads that emphasize the car's sleek design and advanced technology, while a company targeting families might emphasize safety and spaciousness.

In media studies, class refers to the social and economic status of individuals and groups within society. This includes factors such as income, education, occupation, and social standing, and is often classified into categories such as working class, middle class, and upper class.

Media representations of class can have a significant impact on how different social groups are perceived and valued in society. These representations can include stereotypes, such as the working-class individual being portrayed as uneducated and uncultured, or the upper-class individual being portrayed as wealthy and sophisticated.

Media producers often use demographic data to identify and target specific audience segments based on their class, as well as other factors such as age, gender, and ethnicity. This can be seen in advertising campaigns that are specifically designed to appeal to certain social groups, or in television programs and films that are created to reflect the values and lifestyles of different classes.

Media is created for target audiences by considering the specific characteristics of that audience. Their producers conduct research to gather information about their target audience's age, gender, ethnicity, socio-economic status, and interests, among other things.

They use this information to create content that will appeal to their target audience, using specific codes and conventions. For example the use of particular music or visual effects that are known to be popular with a particular demographic.

Class is a social construct that can be defined in different ways and can intersect with other factors such as race, ethnicity, gender, and geography, among others. Media content may be created to appeal to different classes, but this does not necessarily mean that people from different classes will consume media in a uniform way. Furthermore, media content may have unintended effects on audiences and contribute to the perpetuation of stereotypes and inequalities. It's important to approach the issue of class in media with sensitivity and critical thinking, and to avoid reinforcing stereotypes or stigmatizing certain groups.

In media studies, the concepts of social class are often simplified into three main categories: upper class, middle class, and working class. However, this is not to suggest that there are no lower classes or in-betweens. There are certainly individuals who fall outside of these three categories, and there are many different ways to analyze and interpret social class. It's important to recognize that class is a complex and multifaceted concept that can be defined in various ways, depending on the context and perspective.

The following are examples of different media targeting different class:

i) The Upper class:
- Financial Times newspaper
- Luxury lifestyle magazines (e.g. Robb Report, Tatler)
- High-end fashion advertising campaigns (e.g. Chanel, Dior)
- Art house films (e.g. Merchant Ivory productions)

ii) The Middle class:
- The Guardian newspaper
- Lifestyle magazines (e.g. Good Housekeeping, Country Living)
- Mainstream films and TV shows (e.g. Game of Thrones, Friends)
- Popular music genres (e.g. rock, pop)

iii) The Working class:
- The Sun newspaper
- Tabloid newspapers (e.g. Daily Mirror, Daily Star)
- Soap operas (e.g. Coronation Street, Eastenders)
- Reality TV shows (e.g. Big Brother, The X Factor)
- Sports coverage (e.g. Match of the Day, Sky Sports News)

Again, Social class is a complex and sometimes fluid concept, and not everyone will neatly fit into one category.

Media can also be targeted towards demographic and age. For example, Children's media: Shows like Sesame Street, Dora the Explorer, and Paw Patrol are designed to appeal to young children, with simple storylines and bright colours.

Teen media: TV shows like Riverdale and 13 Reasons Why, and movies like The Fault in Our Stars and Twilight are aimed at a teenage audience, dealing with themes like young love, coming of age, and teenage angst.

Adult media: TV shows like Game of Thrones and Breaking Bad, and movies like The Godfather and The Shawshank Redemption are geared towards an adult audience, with complex storylines and mature themes.

Media for different genders include the following:

Women's media: Magazines like Cosmopolitan and Vogue are geared towards a female audience, with articles about fashion, beauty, and relationships.

Men's media: Magazines like GQ and Men's Health are targeted towards men, with articles about style, fitness, and sex.

Gender-neutral media: TV shows like Friends and The Office have broad appeal, with storylines and humour that can be enjoyed by people of all genders.

Psychometrics and its use in Media

Psychometrics is the study of psychological measurement, including the measurement of personality traits, intelligence, and attitudes. It can be used to analyze and understand the Behaviours, preferences, and attitudes of audiences.

For example, the use of psychometric data to create targeted advertising campaigns that appeal to specific groups of people based on their interests and attitudes. Psychometric analysis to also used to understand which types of content are most likely to be successful with different audiences, and to tailor their programming or marketing strategies accordingly.

In addition, it can also be used to measure the effectiveness of media campaigns and to track audience engagement over time. By measuring factors such as click-through rates, social media engagement, and viewer feedback, media companies can gain insights into which types of content are resonating with their audiences and adjust their strategies accordingly.

Sample Examination Questions

- Analyse the representation of gender in a film you have studied and explain how it appeals to its target audience.
- Discuss the ways in which online news websites have changed the production and consumption of news.
- Compare and contrast the use of sound in two different film genres.
- Evaluate the impact of social media on the advertising industry.
- Analyse the use of camera shots and angles in a TV programme you have studied.
- Evaluate the use of special effects in a recent blockbuster film.
- Discuss the relationship between news values and the presentation of news in a newspaper.
- Analyse the marketing strategies used for a video game, focusing on the target audience.
- Compare and contrast the representation of ethnicity in two different films.
- Evaluate the effectiveness of the advertising campaign for a recent product, focusing on the use of media platforms.
- Note: These are just some examples of potential GCSE Media examination questions, and they may vary depending on the specific exam board and curriculum.
- How has the representation of gender changed in the media over the last decade? Refer to specific examples from different media forms to support your answer.
- Analyse the construction of a music video of your choice. Consider the use of camera, editing, sound, and any other relevant features in your analysis.
- To what extent do media texts create, reinforce, and challenge stereotypes? Refer to examples from a range of media forms to support your answer.
- Explain the difference between high culture and popular culture. Refer to specific examples from both types of culture to support your answer.
- How does the use of social media affect the way in which news is reported and consumed? Refer to specific examples to support your answer.

GCSE Media Revision Study Guide

- Choose a media product of your choice and explain how it appeals to its target audience. Consider the use of representation, narrative, and other relevant features in your answer.
- Analyse the use of sound in a film of your choice. Consider the use of music, sound effects, and any other relevant features in your analysis.
- Explain how media institutions use marketing and advertising to promote their products. Refer to specific examples to support your answer.
- To what extent does censorship limit freedom of expression in the media? Refer to specific examples to support your answer.
- Choose a media campaign of your choice and explain how it uses various media forms to convey its message. Consider the use of advertising, social media, and other relevant forms of media in your answer.
- How does the use of camera angles contribute to the meaning and representation of a media text? Use examples from a media text of your choice.
- Analyse the representation of gender in a media text of your choice. How does the media text challenge or reinforce traditional gender stereotypes?
- Evaluate the impact of social media on traditional news reporting. Use examples to support your argument.
- To what extent does the use of colour contribute to the overall meaning and representation of a media text? Discuss with reference to a media text of your choice.
- How does the use of sound contribute to the audience's understanding and experience of a media text? Use examples from a media text of your choice.
- Analyse the ways in which a media text of your choice constructs a particular ethnic or national identity. How does this contribute to the overall meaning of the text?
- Evaluate the role of marketing and promotion in the success of a media text. Use examples from a media text of your choice.
- To what extent does the use of narrative structure contribute to the audience's engagement with a media text? Discuss with reference to a media text of your choice.
- Analyse the representation of age in a media text of your choice. How does the media text challenge or reinforce traditional age stereotypes?

- Evaluate the impact of technological advancements on media production and distribution. Use examples to support your argument.
- Analyze the representation of a particular social group in a media text of your choice.
- Compare and contrast the use of sound in two media texts from different genres.
- Evaluate the impact of a particular media technology on the audience.
- To what extent do media institutions shape the media products that are produced?
- Analyze the use of camera shots and angles in a film or TV program of your choice.
- Discuss the role of the media in shaping cultural values and beliefs.
- Evaluate the impact of digital technology on the media industry.
- Analyze the representation of gender in a media text of your choice.
- Compare and contrast the use of lighting in two media texts from different time periods.
- Evaluate the effectiveness of marketing strategies used by media institutions to promote their products.

Thanks for purchasing this book and good luck in your examinations.

Printed in Great Britain
by Amazon